SECOND EDITION

Twisted Network Programming
Essentials

Jessica McKellar and Abe Fettig

O'REILLY®

Beijing · Cambridge · Farnham · Köln · Sebastopol · Tokyo

Twisted Network Programming Essentials, Second Edition

by Jessica McKellar and Abe Fettig

Copyright © 2013 Jessica McKellar. All rights reserved.

Printed in the United States of America.

Published by O'Reilly Media, Inc., 1005 Gravenstein Highway North, Sebastopol, CA 95472.

O'Reilly books may be purchased for educational, business, or sales promotional use. Online editions are also available for most titles (*http://my.safaribooksonline.com*). For more information, contact our corporate/institutional sales department: 800-998-9938 or *corporate@oreilly.com*.

Editor: Meghan Blanchette	**Indexer:** Bob Pfahler
Production Editor: Christopher Hearse	**Cover Designer:** Randy Comer
Copyeditor: Rachel Head	**Interior Designer:** David Futato
Proofreader: Amanda Kersey	**Illustrator:** Rebecca Demarest

March 2013:   Second Edition

Revision History for the Second Edition:

2013-03-11:   First release

See *http://oreilly.com/catalog/errata.csp?isbn=9781449326111* for release details.

ISBN: 978-1-449-32611-1

[LSI]

Table of Contents

Part I.   An Introduction to Twisted

Part II. Building Production-Grade Twisted Services

Part III. More Protocols and More Practice

Foreword to the First Edition

"My name is Ozymandius, king of kings:
Look on my words, ye Mighty, and despair!"
Nothing beside remains. Round the decay
Of that colossal wreck, boundless and bare
The lone and level sands stretch far away.

—Percy Bysshe Shelly, "Ozymandius"

As the Twisted project's originator and nominal leader—and as someone who is not being paid for writing this—I can very honestly say that this is a fine book, and it has made me proud of what I've started. You now hold in your hands a wondrous key that contains the knowledge to unlock a very powerful software system—a software system borne of a consistent, methodical vision; a vision half a decade in realization and hundreds of man-years in implementation; a vision for a video game that has yet to be written, called "Divunal."

I have been lauded many times for my role in Twisted's creation, and in this foreword I will attempt to disabuse you of the notion that any of it was on purpose. Not only was it an accident, but neither I, nor anyone else, has made one iota of progress towards my original goal of writing a game.

When I was eight years old, I decided I wanted to be a writer. I was going to write video games just like my favorite ones, the text-based games from Infocom. They were like books, but better. I knew how to write already—at a fourth-grade level, or so I'm told—and all I needed to figure out was the part where the computer wrote back. Lucky for you nobody thought to tell me how hard that step between the input and the output was, or Twisted would be a series of detective novels instead of a Python program.

Tolkien said it best: "The tale grew in the telling," and I'll say it worse: the code grew in the hacking. Twisted began over a decade after my aforementioned first plunge into the netherworld of software, as a solitary attempt to create a networking subsystem for a small online fantasy world. Since then, it has become an ongoing community quest to unify all manner of asynchronous communications. This book will take you on an adventure through Twisted for the Web, Twisted for email, Twisted for chat, and of course, Twisted for whatever new kind of networked application you want to dream up—maybe even an online video game.

Much as the tale of Twisted has grown and changed, its origins still have a profound effect on its nature, and on its future. Having origins in an eclectic[1] problem domain has attracted an eclectic[2] audience. The community in the online support forum engages in discussions that are "often funny." To put it more directly: we're weird.

"Weird" is a badge I have long worn with pride, dear reader, so please take it as a compliment that I bestow it upon you. You're not simply non-average, you're better than average. Almost by definition, Twisted hackers are the ones for whom "good enough" isn't good enough. You are the web programmers who can't use their operating system's stock HTTP daemon because you need more power and more control over how it's run; the chat developers who aren't content with chatting on a perfectly working network just because it doesn't support some cool new features you want; the (dare I say it?) gamers who aren't content with the market's offerings of online games. You want to create something newer, different, better. To build higher than those who have come before, because you are building not merely upon the shoulders of giants, but upon the apex of an acrobatic balancing act of giants, or more literally an interlocking network of frameworks and libraries for different tasks, rather than just one at a time.

Twisted will let you do that, by letting you leverage code written by far more and far better programmers than I. Twisted provides a common method for that code to cooperate, which means you can use all of that code without performing a complex integration pass. In this spirit, I'd like to invite you to release your Twisted-based projects, or the infrastructure components of them, as open source software, so that we might together build a Twisted commons upon which many more fantastic applications will be built.

Don't mistake this friendly vision for altruism, however. I didn't have anything to do with the start of the Free Software or Open Source movements, respectively, but they came along at a convenient time for me. This feeling of share-and-share-alike has been a feature of the Twisted community since day one, but not because I care about sharing.[3] It is because—I may have mentioned this—I want to write a video game one day. A game that effortlessly connects to the Web and to your email, that politely requests that you play when you have time, and that reminds you to get back to work when you do not.

---

1. And difficult! Making an online game work properly is *hard*.

2. And intelligent! People who solve unusual problems are always learning.

3. Caution for the humorless: this is a joke. I am not actually an enemy of freedom. Still, there is some truth to this.

You see, the majority of Twisted's core developers, including myself, suffer from Attention Deficit Disorder. This malady is the grease that makes the magic wheels of integration turn. While most developers—sane developers—would be content to write a perfectly good web server that could work only as a web server and leave it at that, we are always afraid we'll suddenly lose interest and need a chat application instead—or maybe it should be a mail server? Hey, there's a squirrel! I don't like this song.

What was I saying? Oh yes. The essence of Twisted is apparently paradoxical. Created on a whim by crazed eccentrics, designed to be a toy, and yet powerful enough to drive massive email systems, high-traffic web sites, transaction-processing systems, and inventory management applications.

However, the paradox is an illusion. People produce the best work when they are working and having fun at the same time. It takes a sense of humor to call yourself a crazed eccentric (whether it's true or not). You have to have a sense of fun to try and build a toy. In enjoying ourselves, we have brought to life a system that many of us have tried and been unable to create in more serious surroundings.

So, when I look out upon the "lone and level sands" of Divunal, a game whose incarnation today is little more than its name, I am not concerned. I am having a good time with Twisted. With this book in hand, I have no doubt that you will, too.

—Matthew "the Glyph" Lefkowitz
CTO at Divmod, Inc.
(not a game company)
(yet)
August 2005

Preface

This book is about Twisted, an open source, event-driven networking engine written in Python.

Twisted supports many common transport and application layer protocols, including TCP, UDP, SSL/TLS, HTTP, IMAP, SSH, IRC, and FTP. Like the language in which it is written, it is "batteries-included"; Twisted comes with client and server implementations for all of its protocols, as well as utilities that make it easy to configure and deploy production-grade Twisted applications from the command line.

Twisted includes both high- and low-level tools for building performant, cross-platform applications. You can deploy a web or mail server with just a few lines of code, or you can write your own protocol from scratch. At every level, Twisted provides a tested, RFC-conforming, extensible API that makes it possible to rapidly develop powerful network software.

In keeping with the spirit of the O'Reilly Essentials series, this book is not about torturing you with the nitty-gritty details of specific networking protocols, or with exhaustively documenting Twisted's APIs. For a comprehensive treatment of how to use Twisted to build applications for a particular protocol, please get your footing with this book and then consult the official documentation.

Instead, the goal of this book is to give you fluency in the primitives Twisted provides and the idioms that it uses to build network clients and servers. It starts with an introduction to the underlying event-driven model and a big-picture view of Twisted as a framework, focusing on simple, self-contained examples that you can play with and extend as you explore Twisted's APIs. Where possible, the client and server examples are written so they can be run together.

After reading this book, you will have the tools and conceptual background to build any event-driven client or server application you need, not just for the protocols that are a part of Twisted and covered in this book, but also for new protocols that you build using Twisted's primitives.

Why Use Twisted?

Why should you use Twisted instead of some other networking library or framework? Here are a few compelling reasons. Twisted is:

Python-powered
> Twisted is written in Python, a powerful, object-oriented, interpreted language. Python is a language that inspires great enthusiasm among its fans, and for good reason. It's a joy to program in Python, which is easy to write, easy to read, and easy to run. And because Python is cross-platform, you can run the same Twisted application on Linux, Windows, Unix, and Mac OS X.

Asynchronous and event-based
> Synchronous network libraries leave developers with a painful choice: either allow the application to become unresponsive during network operations, or introduce the additional complexity of threading. Twisted's event-based, asynchronous framework makes it possible to write applications that stay responsive while processing events from multiple network connections, without using threads.

Full-featured
> Twisted includes an amazing amount of functionality. Mail, web, news, chat, DNS, SSH, Telnet, RPC, database access, and more—it's all there, ready for you to use.

Flexible and extensible
> Twisted provides high-level classes to let you get started quickly. But you'll never find yourself limited by the way things work out of the box. If you need advanced functionality, or if you need to customize the way a protocol works, you can. You can also write your own protocol implementation, to control every byte sent over the wire.

Open source
> Twisted is free, both as in beer and as in freedom. It includes full source code and is released under a liberal license. Want to distribute all or part of Twisted with your application? You're welcome to do so, with no obligations to release your own code or pay any licensing fees. Want to get a better understanding of how an object in Twisted works? Take a look at the source. And when you get to the point where you're developing your own improvements and extensions to Twisted, you can contribute them to the community for the benefit of others.

Community-backed
> Twisted has an active community of developers and users. If you run into a problem, you'll find many fellow developers ready to help on one of the Twisted mailing lists (see "Finding Answers to Your Questions" on page 9, in Chapter 1). Or you can drop into the *#twisted* IRC channel, where the chances are good you'll be able to start a live conversation with the very person who wrote the code you're having trouble with.

An integration-friendly platform

A Twisted application can share data between several different services within the same process. This makes integration tasks a snap. You can write an SMTP-to-XMLRPC proxy, an SSH server that lets you update a website, or a web discussion board that includes an NNTP interface. If you need to transfer data between systems that don't speak the same protocol, Twisted will make your job a whole lot easier.

What This Book Covers

This book does not attempt to exhaustively document every module and class available for the Twisted framework. Instead, it focuses on presenting practical examples of the most common tasks that developers building network applications face. This book will also help you to understand the key concepts and design patterns used in Twisted applications.

This book has three parts:

Learning Twisted basics through building basic clients and servers

This part covers installing Twisted, an architectural overview of the framework, and building basic TCP clients and servers. We then apply the primitives and idioms from the chapters on basic applications to a variety of client and server examples for a particular protocol, HTTP.

Building production-grade servers

At this point, well-practiced with basic clients and servers, we focus on deploying these applications in a robust and standardized fashion using the Twisted application infrastructure. This part also adds to our repertoire common components of production-grade servers: logging, database access, authentication, using threads and processes in a Twisted-safe way, and testing.

More practice through examples from other protocols

For more practice, to give a sense of Twisted's breadth, and to cover many popular uses of Twisted, the final part of the book explores clients and servers for IRC, various mail protocols, and SSH.

Conventions Used in This Book

This book uses standard typographical conventions to highlight different types of text. You'll see the following font styles used:

Italic

Used for emphasis, to highlight technical terms the first time they appear, and for commands, packages, filenames, directories, and URLs

Constant width
>   Used for code samples, and for the names of variables, classes, objects, and functions when they are used within the main text of the book

Constant width bold
>   Shows user input at the command line and interactive prompts

Constant width bold italic
>   Shows placeholder user input that you should replace with something that makes sense for you

     This icon signifies a tip, suggestion, or general note.

     This icon indicates a warning or caution.

What You'll Need

This book assumes a familiarity with programming in Python. If you're looking for a good introduction to Python, check out *Learning Python*, by Mark Lutz (O'Reilly), or *Dive Into Python*, by Mark Pilgrim (Apress). You should have a Linux, Mac OS X, or Windows computer with Python version 2.6 or 2.7 installed. Python 2.6 is included in Mac OS X 10.6 ("Snow Leopard") and higher and in many Linux distributions. If you don't already have Python installed, you can download it for free from the *Python home page*.

Changes Since the Previous Edition

The first edition of *Twisted Networking Essentials* was released in 2005. Since then, networking protocols have come in and out of fashion, and Twisted's APIs have evolved and matured. This second edition builds upon the excellent foundation first edition author Abe Fettig crafted by trimming off aged protocols and Twisted APIs and covering more Twisted subprojects and features.

In particular, this edition removes the chapter on NNTP and adds chapters on building IRC clients and servers and testing your Twisted applications using the Trial framework. The sections on deploying production-grade services using the Twisted application infrastructure have been significantly expanded. In addition to a discussion and examples of Twisted applications and Twisted plugins, logging, working with databases, and using threads and processes all now get more coverage in their own chapters.

The focus of this book has also been sharpened to give you fluency in Twisted's primitives and idioms with minimal distraction from the nitty-gritty details of specific protocols. Almost all of the examples have been streamlined, and where reasonable, reworked so that you have client and server pairs that can be run together to maximize experimentation value. Also, as part of building a solid conceptual foundation, the section on Deferreds, a frequent source of confusion and frustration for developers new to event-driven programming, has been expanded into its own chapter with many more examples.

Since the structure and many of the examples have changed, it is hard to give a short and complete enumeration of the differences between this edition and the last. I hope this has given you some idea, though, and I welcome your thoughts and feedback.

Portions of Chapters 2, 3, and 6 were adapted from the author's chapter on *Twisted for The Architecture of Open Source Applications, Volume II* under a Creative Commons Attribution 3.0 Unported license. You can find out more about this book at The Architecture of Open Source Applications home page (*http://www.aosabook.org/*) and about this license at the Creative Commons website (*https://creativecommons.org/licenses/by/3.0/*).

Using Code Examples

This book is here to help you get your job done. In general, if this book includes code examples, you may use the code in your programs and documentation. You do not need to contact us for permission unless you're reproducing a significant portion of the code. For example, writing a program that uses several chunks of code from this book does not require permission. Selling or distributing a CD-ROM of examples from O'Reilly books does require permission. Answering a question by citing this book and quoting example code does not require permission. Incorporating a significant amount of example code from this book into your product's documentation does require permission.

We appreciate, but do not require, attribution. An attribution usually includes the title, author, publisher, and ISBN. For example: "*Twisted Network Programming Essentials*, Second Edition, by Jessica McKellar and Abe Fettig (O'Reilly). Copyright 2013 Jessica McKellar, 978-1-4493-2611-1."

If you feel your use of code examples falls outside fair use or the permission given above, feel free to contact us at *permissions@oreilly.com*.

Safari® Books Online

 Safari Books Online (*www.safaribooksonline.com*) is an on-demand digital library that delivers expert content in both book and video form from the world's leading authors in technology and business.

Technology professionals, software developers, web designers, and business and creative professionals use Safari Books Online as their primary resource for research, problem solving, learning, and certification training.

Safari Books Online offers a range of product mixes and pricing programs for organizations, government agencies, and individuals. Subscribers have access to thousands of books, training videos, and prepublication manuscripts in one fully searchable database from publishers like O'Reilly Media, Prentice Hall Professional, Addison-Wesley Professional, Microsoft Press, Sams, Que, Peachpit Press, Focal Press, Cisco Press, John Wiley & Sons, Syngress, Morgan Kaufmann, IBM Redbooks, Packt, Adobe Press, FT Press, Apress, Manning, New Riders, McGraw-Hill, Jones & Bartlett, Course Technology, and dozens more. For more information about Safari Books Online, please visit us online.

How to Contact Us

Please address comments and questions concerning this book to the publisher:

> O'Reilly Media, Inc.
> 1005 Gravenstein Highway North
> Sebastopol, CA 95472
> 800-998-9938 (in the United States or Canada)
> 707-829-0515 (international or local)
> 707-829-0104 (fax)

We have a web page for this book, where we list errata, examples, and any additional information. You can access this page at *http://oreil.ly/twisted-network-2e*.

To comment or ask technical questions about this book, send email to *bookquestions@oreilly.com*.

For more information about our books, courses, conferences, and news, see our website at *http://www.oreilly.com*.

Find us on Facebook: *http://facebook.com/oreilly*

Follow us on Twitter: *http://twitter.com/oreillymedia*

Watch us on YouTube: *http://www.youtube.com/oreillymedia*

Acknowledgments

Twisted was my first-ever experience with open source contribution. I am so grateful that as a naive and clueless intern way back when, Glyph, JP, Itamar, and others patiently guided me through the contribution process and invested their time in making me a core developer for the project. What I've learned from this wonderful community continues to influence my open source and software engineering sensibilities and discipline today, and I strive to give back half as much as they've given me.

Thank you Christopher Armstrong, Andrew Bennetts, Jean-Paul Calderone, Thomas Herve, Kevin Horn, Laurens Van Houtven, James Knight, Jonathan Lange, Glyph Lefkowitz, Ying Li, Duncan McGreggor, Ashwini Oruganti, David Reid, Allen Short, David Sturgis, Kevin Turner, and the many other contributors who have helped me and who steward Twisted, support new contributors, help users, write code, write documentation, write tests, and maintain the infrastructure for Twisted. It is truly a group effort.

Thank you Adam Fletcher and Laurens Van Houtven for providing technical reviews for this edition. I appreciate your tolerance for my propensity for deadline-driven development. Your feedback has made this book much stronger. Thank you to my editor Meghan Blanchette, whose stuck with and pushed me patiently as at each deadline I tried to creep in one...last...tweak...I promise.

PART I

An Introduction to Twisted

CHAPTER 1

Getting Started

Before you can start developing applications using Twisted, you'll need to download and install Twisted and its dependencies. This chapter walks you through the installation process on various operating systems. It also shows you how to add the Twisted utilities to your path, familiarize yourself with the Twisted documentation, and get answers to your questions from the Twisted community.

These instructions assume that you are familiar with Python and, in the case of source installations, comfortable navigating and installing packages from the command line.

Twisted requires Python 2.6 or 2.7. Support for Python 3.0 is in progress at the time of this writing.

Installing Twisted

First things first: you need to get Twisted installed on your computer. Downloads and instructions for installing Twisted on various operating systems can be found on the Twisted home page (*http://twistedmatrix.com*), with additional instructions and links to older releases at this Twisted page (*http://bit.ly/XSAPKP*). To enable additional functionality in Twisted, you'll have to install a couple of optional packages as well.

You can find everything you need on the Twisted website, but if you'd like you can also browse this page on PyPI (*http://bit.ly/XSARm5*) for the source, Windows installers, and download statistics.

Installation on Linux

All of the popular Linux distributions maintain a *python-twisted* package as well as packaged versions of Twisted's dependencies. To install Twisted on a *dpkg*-based system, run:

```
apt-get install python-twisted
```

On an *rpm*-based system, run:

```
yum install python-twisted
```

That's it! You now have a functional Twisted installation. If you want to use some of Twisted's extra features or learn about installing from source on Linux, read on. Otherwise, you can skip to "Testing Your Installation" on page 7.

More package options and optional dependencies

Twisted also maintains an Ubuntu PPA at the "Twisted-dev" team Launchpad page (*http://bit.ly/XSARCx*) with packages for the latest Twisted version on all active Ubuntu releases.

If you'll be using Twisted's SSL or SSH features, you can find the pyOpenSSL and PyCrypto packages as *python-openssl* and *python-crypto*, respectively.

If Twisted isn't packaged for your platform, or you want a newer version that hasn't been packaged for your distribution release yet, please refer to the instructions below in "Installing from Source" on page 5.

Installation on Windows

Twisted prepares 32-bit and 64-bit MSI and EXE installers for Windows. If you're not sure which version you need, the 32-bit MSI will always work.

Download and run both the Twisted installer and the `zope.interface` installer from the sidebar on the Twisted home page (*http://bit.ly/XSAO9X*).

That's it! You now have a functional Twisted installation. If you want to use some of Twisted's extra features or learn about installing from source on Windows, read on. Otherwise, take a look at the section below on adding Twisted utilities to your PATH, then skip ahead to "Testing Your Installation" on page 7.

Optional dependencies

If you'll be using Twisted's SSL or SSH features, please also install pyOpenSSL and PyCrypto. You can find Windows installers for these packages at this Twisted download page (*http://bit.ly/XSAPKP*).

Adding Twisted utilities to your PATH

Twisted includes a number of utilities that you'll use to run and test your code. On Windows, the location of these utilities is not automatically added to your PATH, so to run them you have to supply the full path to the program. To make life easier, add these utilities to your PATH so that you can run them by name instead.

Twisted's utilities will be installed in the Python *Scripts* directory, typically in a location such as *C:\Python27\Scripts*. Edit your PATH to include the path to the *Scripts* directory.

After adding the *Scripts* directory to your PATH, you should be able to run the Twisted utilities by name. Test your changes by running:

```
trial.py
```

at a new command prompt. The usage message for Twisted's *Trial* unit testing framework should be displayed.

To avoid typing the *.py* extension for these utilities, add '.py' to your PATHEXT environment variable. After doing that, at a new command prompt you should be able to run:

```
trial
```

by itself.

Installation on OS X

OS X versions 10.5 and later ship with a version of Twisted. If you are running an older version of OS X, or you want a newer version of Twisted, please refer to the instructions in the next section on installing from source. Otherwise, that's it—you have a functional Twisted installation! If you want to use some of Twisted's extra features or learn about installing from source on OS X, read on. Otherwise, you can skip to "Testing Your Installation" on page 7.

Optional dependencies

If you'll be using Twisted's SSL or SSH features, you'll need pyOpenSSL and PyCrypto (*http://bit.ly/XSAPKP*), respectively. OS X ships with pyOpenSSL.

Installing from Source

If you're on an operating system for which no Twisted binary packages are available or you want to run a newer version of Twisted than has been packaged for your system, you'll need to install from source.

Required Dependencies

Twisted has two required dependencies.

Installing a C compiler

Since installing Twisted from source involves compiling C code, on OS X or Windows you'll need to install a C compiler before you can install Twisted.

Installing zope.interface

When installing from source, before you can use Twisted, you'll also need to install zope.interface, which you can download from the sidebar on theTwisted home page (*http://bit.ly/XSAO9X*).

Installing Twisted from a Release Tarball

To install the latest Twisted release from source, first download the release tarball from this Twisted download page (*http://bit.ly/XSAPKP*).

After downloading the tarball, uncompress and unpack it with a command like:

```
tar xvfj Twisted-12.0.0.tar.bz2
```

Then *cd* into the resulting directory and run:

```
python setup.py install
```

with administrative privileges. This will install the Twisted library and utilities.

Installing Twisted from a Source Checkout

If you'd like to use the development version of Twisted, you can check out the Twisted Subversion (SVN) repository.

You may first need to install a Subversion client. On a *dpkg*-based system you can use:

```
apt-get install subversion
```

and on an *rpm*-based system you can use:

```
yum install subversion
```

On Windows, one popular GUI SVN client is TortoiseSVN, which you can download from the Tigris.org page on TortoiseSVN (*http://bit.ly/XSASqc*). Recent versions of OS X come with Subversion installed.

Once you have a Subversion client installed, check out the Twisted repository with:

```
svn checkout svn://svn.twistedmatrix.com/svn/Twisted/trunk TwistedTrunk
```

Then *cd* into the resulting *TwistedTrunk* directory and run:

```
python setup.py install
```

with administrative privileges. This will install the Twisted library and utilities.

Installing Optional Dependencies from Source

If pyOpenSSL or PyCrypto binaries are not available for your operating system, you can download and compile the source packages from the pyOpenSSL Launchpad page (*http://bit.ly/XSASGx*) and the Dlitz.net PyCrypto page (*http://bit.ly/XSATKy*), respectively.

Testing Your Installation

To verify that the installation worked and that you have the desired version of Twisted installed, import the *twisted* module from a Python prompt:

```
$ python
Python 2.6.6 (r266:84292, Dec 26 2010, 22:31:48)
[GCC 4.4.5] on linux2
Type "help", "copyright", "credits" or "license" for more information.
>>> import twisted
>>> twisted.__version__
'12.0.0'
>>>
```

If the *import twisted* statement runs with no errors, you have a working Twisted installation.

If you've installed pyOpenSSL to use Twisted's SSL features, you can test that that installation worked with:

```
>>> import OpenSSL
>>> import twisted.internet.ssl
>>> twisted.internet.ssl.SSL
```

If you don't see any errors, you've successfully added SSL support to your Twisted installation.

If you've installed PyCrypto to use Twisted's SSH features, you can test that that installation worked with:

```
>>> import Crypto
>>> import twisted.conch.ssh.transport
>>> twisted.conch.ssh.transport.md5
```

If you don't see any errors, you've successfully added SSH support to your Twisted installation.

 If you have more than one version of Python installed, keep in mind that Twisted will be installed for only the version of Python you're using when you run *setup.py*. To check your Python version, run *python -V*.

Congratulations—you now have a working Twisted installation and the tools you need to start developing applications using Twisted!

Using the Twisted Documentation

Twisted includes several types of documentation: extensive API documentation, HOW-TOs, tutorials, examples, and manpages. It's a good idea to familiarize yourself with this documentation now so that you'll be able to refer to it during the development process.

API Documentation

A complete API reference can be found on the Twisted website (*http://bit.ly/XSASGF*). The pages in the API documentation are automatically generated from the source code using *lore*, a custom documentation tool developed as part of Twisted.

API references are also maintained for all prior releases. To view the documentation for an older version of Twisted, just replace "current" in the above URL with the appropriate version number, as in this Twisted webpage (*http://bit.ly/XSASWZ*).

Subproject Documentation

Twisted is developed as a set of subprojects, and each subproject has additional documentation in its section of the Twisted site. For example, you can access documentation on the Twisted Core networking libraries (*http://twistedmatrix.com/documents/current/core/*), and documentation on Twisted Web (*http://twistedmatrix.com/documents/current/web/*). You can also check out links to the full list of projects and documentation (*http://bit.ly/XSATu0*).

Within each subproject's documentation, you'll find the following types of information:

HOWTOs
> These documents describe specific features of Twisted and how to use them. The HOWTOs don't cover every part of Twisted, but they can provide a helpful starting point for certain tasks. Included in the HOWTOs is a tutorial called "Twisted from Scratch" that walks through building an extensible, configurable, robustly deployable service in Twisted from scratch.

Examples
> These are examples of short and specific Twisted programs. Like the HOWTOs, these aren't comprehensive but can be an excellent resource when you need a working example of a certain feature. The Twisted Core documentation includes examples of basic TCP, UDP, and SSL servers and clients.

Manual pages
> When you installed Twisted, you also installed manpages for the Twisted utilities. This Twisted page (*http://bit.ly/XSAUhG*) has HTML versions of these manpages.

Finding Answers to Your Questions

If you get stuck or want advice on a project, there are many excellent Twisted community resources you can look to for help.

Mailing Lists

Twisted has two main mailing lists:

twisted-python
> This is a general discussion list for Twisted. It's the main mailing list for asking development questions. It is also the place where Twisted releases and releases for projects that use Twisted are announced. Folks also use this list to organize sprints, discuss tickets, ask for design feedback, and talk about maintaining the Twisted website, Buildbots, and the rest of the project infrastructure.
>
> You can join this list or read the archives (*http://bit.ly/XSAUhO*).

twisted-web
> This is a list for discussion of web technologies related to Twisted.
>
> You can join this list or read the archives (*http://bit.ly/XSAUyf*).

IRC Channels

Twisted users and developers ask questions and get help in the *#twisted* and *#twisted.web* IRC channels on the Freenode network. These are very active channels, but if you don't get an immediate answer on IRC, try sending a message to the appropriate mailing list.

In *#twisted*, you'll find a helpful bot named *kenaan* that sends messages when tickets are opened, put up for review, or resolved, and it can be told to monitor Buildbot builds.

Stack Overflow

The Stack Overflow programming Q & A site has built up a large body of Twisted questions and answers (*http://bit.ly/XSAWWR*).

Twisted Blogs

Twisted developers post sprint reports and release announcements to the Twisted blog (*http://bit.ly/XSAUOJ*).

The personal blogs of Twisted developers are aggregated on Planet Twisted (*http://bit.ly/XSAWX1*).

CHAPTER 2

Building Basic Clients and Servers

The best way to learn about the components of a Twisted application is to dive right into some examples. This chapter will introduce you to the reactor event loop, transports, and protocols through implementations of a few basic TCP servers and clients.

A TCP Echo Server and Client

Skim the code for the TCP echo server and client pair in Examples 2-1 and 2-2. The server's job is to listen for TCP connections on a particular port and echo back anything it receives. The client's job is to connect to the server, send it a message, receive a response, and terminate the connection.

Example 2-1. echoserver.py

```
from twisted.internet import protocol, reactor

class Echo(protocol.Protocol):
    def dataReceived(self, data):
        self.transport.write(data)

class EchoFactory(protocol.Factory):
    def buildProtocol(self, addr):
        return Echo()

reactor.listenTCP(8000, EchoFactory())
reactor.run()
```

Example 2-2. echoclient.py

```
from twisted.internet import reactor, protocol

class EchoClient(protocol.Protocol):
    def connectionMade(self):
        self.transport.write("Hello, world!")
```

```
    def dataReceived(self, data):
        print "Server said:", data
        self.transport.loseConnection()

class EchoFactory(protocol.ClientFactory):
    def buildProtocol(self, addr):
        return EchoClient()

    def clientConnectionFailed(self, connector, reason):
        print "Connection failed."
        reactor.stop()

    def clientConnectionLost(self, connector, reason):
        print "Connection lost."
        reactor.stop()

reactor.connectTCP("localhost", 8000, EchoFactory())
reactor.run()
```

To test this pair of scripts, first run the server in one terminal with *python echoserver.py*. This will start a TCP server listening for connections on port 8000. Then run the client in a second terminal with *python echoclient.py*.

A transcript from the session looks like this:

```
$ python echoserver.py # In Terminal 1

$ python echoclient.py # In Terminal 2
Server said: Hello, world!
Connection lost.
```

Ta-da! You've just completed your first asynchronous, event-driven communication with Twisted. Let's look at each of the components of these scripts in more detail.

Event-Driven Programming

The echo server and echo client are event-driven programs, and more generally Twisted is an event-driven networking engine. What does that mean?

In an event-driven program, program flow is determined by external events. It is characterized by an *event loop* and the use of callbacks to trigger actions when events happen. Contrast this structure with two other common models: *single-threaded* (synchronous) and *multithreaded* programming.

Figure 2-1 summarizes these three models visually by showing the work done by a program over time under each of them. The program has three tasks to complete, each of which blocks while waiting for I/O to finish. Time spent blocking on I/O is grayed out.

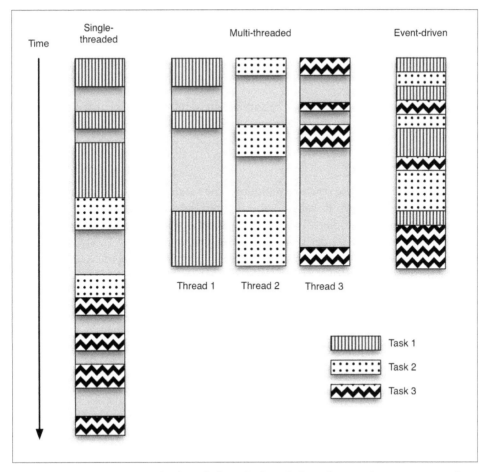

Figure 2-1. Comparing single-threaded, multithreaded, and event-driven program flow

In the single-threaded synchronous version of the program, tasks are performed serially. If one task blocks on I/O, all of the other tasks must also wait. Single-threaded programs are thus easy to reason about but can be unnecessarily slow.

In the multithreaded version, the three blocking tasks are performed in separate threads of control, which may run interleaved on one or many processors. This allows progress to be made by some threads while others are blocking on resources and is often more time-efficient than the analogous synchronous program. However, one has to write code that protects shared resources that could be accessed concurrently from multiple threads, which when implemented improperly can lead to notoriously subtle and painful threading bugs.

The event-driven version of the program interleaves the execution of the three tasks, but in a single thread of control. When performing I/O or other expensive operations, a callback is registered with an event loop, and then execution continues while the I/O completes. The callback describes how to handle an event once it has completed. The event loop polls for events and dispatches them as they arrive to the callbacks that are waiting for them. This allows the program to make progress without the use of additional threads.

Event-driven programs enjoy both the parallelism of multithreaded programs and the ease of reasoning of single-threaded programs.

The Reactor

The core of Twisted is the reactor event loop. The reactor knows about network, file-system, and timer events. It waits on and demultiplexes these events and dispatches them to waiting event handlers. Twisted takes care of abstracting away platform-specific behavior and using the underlying nonblocking APIs correctly. Twisted presents a common interface to the various event sources so that responding to events anywhere in the network stack is easy.

The reactor essentially accomplishes the following:

```
while True:
    timeout = time_until_next_timed_event()
    events = wait_for_events(timeout)
    events += timed_events_until(now())
    for event in events:
        event.process()
```

In our echo server and client from Examples 2-1 and 2-2, the reactor's listenTCP and connectTCP methods take care of registering callbacks with the reactor to get notified when data is available to read from a TCP socket on port 8000.

After those callbacks have been registered, we start the reactor's event loop with reactor.run. Once running, the reactor will poll for and dispatch events forever or until reactor.stop is called.

Transports

A *transport* represents the connection between two endpoints communicating over a network. Transports describe connection details: for example, is this connection stream-oriented (like TCP) or datagram-oriented (like UDP)? TCP, UDP, Unix sockets, and serial ports are examples of transports. Transports implement the ITransport interface, which has the following methods:

write
    Write data to the physical connection in a nonblocking manner.

writeSequence
Write a list of strings to the physical connection. Useful when working with line-oriented protocols.

loseConnection
Write all pending data and then close the connection.

getPeer
Get the remote address of the connection.

getHost
Like getPeer, but returns the address of the local side of the connection.

In the echo server and client examples from earlier, the two endpoints send each other data using their transport's write method. The client terminates the TCP connection after receiving a response from the server by calling loseConnection.

Protocols

Protocols describe how to process network events asynchronously. Twisted maintains implementations for many popular application protocols, including HTTP, Telnet, DNS, and IMAP. Protocols implement the IProtocol interface, which has the following methods:

makeConnection
Create a connection between two endpoints across a transport.

connectionMade
Called when a connection to another endpoint is made.

dataReceived
Called when data is received across a transport.

connectionLost
Called when the connection is shut down.

In our echo server, we create our own Echo protocol by subclassing protocol.Protocol. To echo data back to the client, we take the data received from the client and simply write it back out through the transport in dataReceived.

In the echo client, we create our own EchoClient protocol by subclassing protocol.Protocol. The call to connectTCP creates a TCP connection to the server on port 8000 and registers callbacks for the various stages of the connection. For example, a callback is registered to invoke dataReceived when new data is available on the transport. Once the connection is established, we write data out to the server through the transport in connectionMade. When we receive data back from the server in dataReceived, we print that data and close the TCP connection.

Protocol Factories

A new instance of our Echo protocol class is instantiated for every connection and goes away when the connection terminates. This means that persistent configuration information is not saved in the protocol.

Persistent configuration information is instead kept in an EchoFactory class, which inherits from protocol.Factory in the server and protocol.ClientFactory in the client. A factory's buildProtocol method creates a protocol for each new connection, which gets passed to the reactor to register callbacks.

Decoupling Transports and Protocols

A major design decision in Twisted is that transports and protocols are completely decoupled. This decoupling makes it easy for many protocols to reuse the same type of transport. It is also hugely important for testing: to test a protocol implementation you can have it use a mock transport that simply writes data to a string for inspection. You'll experience this first-hand in Chapter 11.

A TCP Quote Server and Client

Let's reiterate some of the core ideas discussed in the previous sections with a slightly more complicated quote exchange service.

The quote server in Example 2-3 is seeded with an initial quote. Upon receiving a quote from a client, it will send the client its current quote and store the client's quote to share with the next client. It also keeps track of the number of concurrent client connections.

The client in Example 2-4 creates several TCP connections, each of which exchanges a quote with the server.

Example 2-3. quoteserver.py

```
from twisted.internet.protocol import Factory
from twisted.internet import reactor, protocol

class QuoteProtocol(protocol.Protocol):
    def __init__(self, factory):
        self.factory = factory

    def connectionMade(self):
        self.factory.numConnections += 1

    def dataReceived(self, data):
        print "Number of active connections: %d" % (
            self.factory.numConnections,)
        print "> Received: ``%s''\n>  Sending: ``%s''" % (
            data, self.getQuote())
        self.transport.write(self.getQuote())
```

```
            self.updateQuote(data)

    def connectionLost(self, reason):
        self.factory.numConnections -= 1

    def getQuote(self):
        return self.factory.quote

    def updateQuote(self, quote):
        self.factory.quote = quote

class QuoteFactory(Factory):
    numConnections = 0

    def __init__(self, quote=None):
        self.quote = quote or "An apple a day keeps the doctor away"

    def buildProtocol(self, addr):
        return QuoteProtocol(self)

reactor.listenTCP(8000, QuoteFactory())
reactor.run()
```

Example 2-4. quoteclient.py

```
from twisted.internet import reactor, protocol

class QuoteProtocol(protocol.Protocol):
    def __init__(self, factory):
        self.factory = factory

    def connectionMade(self):
        self.sendQuote()

    def sendQuote(self):
        self.transport.write(self.factory.quote)

    def dataReceived(self, data):
        print "Received quote:", data
        self.transport.loseConnection()

class QuoteClientFactory(protocol.ClientFactory):
    def __init__(self, quote):
        self.quote = quote

    def buildProtocol(self, addr):
        return QuoteProtocol(self)

    def clientConnectionFailed(self, connector, reason):
        print 'connection failed:', reason.getErrorMessage()
        maybeStopReactor()

    def clientConnectionLost(self, connector, reason):
```

```
        print 'connection lost:', reason.getErrorMessage()
        maybeStopReactor()

def maybeStopReactor():
    global quote_counter
    quote_counter -= 1
    if not quote_counter:
        reactor.stop()

quotes = [
    "You snooze you lose",
    "The early bird gets the worm",
    "Carpe diem"
]
quote_counter = len(quotes)

for quote in quotes:
    reactor.connectTCP('localhost', 8000, QuoteClientFactory(quote))
reactor.run()
```

Start the server in one terminal with *python quoteserver.py* and then run the client in another terminal with *python quoteclient.py*. Transcripts from these sessions will look something like the following—note that because this communication is asynchronous, the order in which connections are made and terminated may vary between runs:

```
$ python quoteserver.py
Number of active connections: 2
> Received: ``You snooze you lose''
>  Sending: ``An apple a day keeps the doctor away.''
Number of active connections: 2
> Received: ``The early bird gets the worm''
>  Sending: ``You snooze you lose''
Number of active connections: 3
> Received: ``Carpe diem''
>  Sending: ``The early bird gets the worm''

$ python quoteclient.py
Received quote: The early bird gets the worm
Received quote: You snooze you lose
connection lost: Connection was closed cleanly.
connection lost: Connection was closed cleanly.
Received quote: Carpe diem
connection lost: Connection was closed cleanly.
```

This quote server and client pair highlight some key points about client/server communication in Twisted:

1. **Persistent protocol state is kept in the factory.**

    Because a new instance of a protocol class is created for each connection, protocols can't contain persistent state; that information must instead be stored in a protocol factory. In the echo server, the number of current connections is stored in numConnections in QuoteFactory.

It is common for a factory's buildProtocol method to do nothing beyond return an instance of a Protocol. For that simple case, Twisted provides a shortcut: instead of implementing buildProtocol, just define a protocol class variable for the factory; the default implementation of buildProtocol will take care of creating an instance of your Protocol and setting a factory attribute on the protocol pointing back to the factory (making it easy for protocol instances to access the shared state stored in the factory).

For example, you could get rid of QuoteProtocol's __init__ method and QuoteFactory could be rewritten as:

```
class QuoteFactory(Factory):
    numConnections = 0
    protocol = QuoteProtocol

    def __init__(self, quote=None):
        self.quote = quote or "An apple a day keeps the doctor away."
```

This is a common idiom in Twisted programs, so keep an eye out for it!

2. **Protocols can retrieve the reason why a connection was terminated.**

   The reason is passed as an argument to clientConnectionLost and clientConnectionFailed. If you run *quoteclient.py* without a server waiting for its connections, you'll get:

```
$ python quoteclient.py
connection failed: Connection was refused by other side...
connection failed: Connection was refused by other side...
connection failed: Connection was refused by other side...
```

3. **Clients can make make many simultaneous connections to a server.**

   To do this, simply call connectTCP repeatedly, as was done in the quote client before starting the reactor.

Lastly, our use of maybeStopReactor is hinting at a general client design issue of how to determine when all of the connections you wanted to make have terminated (often so that you can shut down the reactor). maybeStopReactor gets the job done here, but we'll explore a more idiomatic way of accomplishing this using objects called Deferreds later in the next book.

Protocol State Machines

Protocols typically have different states and can be expressed in client and server code as a state machine. Example 2-5 is a chat server that implements a small state machine. It also subclasses the LineReceiver class, which is a convenience class that makes it easy to write line-based protocols. When using LineReceiver, a client should send messages with sendLine and a server should process received messages in lineReceived.

Example 2-5. chatserver.py

```python
from twisted.internet.protocol import Factory
from twisted.protocols.basic import LineReceiver
from twisted.internet import reactor

class ChatProtocol(LineReceiver):
    def __init__(self, factory):
        self.factory = factory
        self.name = None
        self.state = "REGISTER"

    def connectionMade(self):
        self.sendLine("What's your name?")

    def connectionLost(self, reason):
        if self.name in self.factory.users:
            del self.factory.users[self.name]
            self.broadcastMessage("%s has left the channel." % (self.name,))

    def lineReceived(self, line):
        if self.state == "REGISTER":
            self.handle_REGISTER(line)
        else:
            self.handle_CHAT(line)

    def handle_REGISTER(self, name):
        if name in self.factory.users:
            self.sendLine("Name taken, please choose another.")
            return
        self.sendLine("Welcome, %s!" % (name,))
        self.broadcastMessage("%s has joined the channel." % (name,))
        self.name = name
        self.factory.users[name] = self
        self.state = "CHAT"

    def handle_CHAT(self, message):
        message = "<%s> %s" % (self.name, message)
        self.broadcastMessage(message)

    def broadcastMessage(self, message):
        for name, protocol in self.factory.users.iteritems():
            if protocol != self:
                protocol.sendLine(message)

class ChatFactory(Factory):
    def __init__(self):
        self.users = {}
```

```
    def buildProtocol(self, addr):
        return ChatProtocol(self)

reactor.listenTCP(8000, ChatFactory())
reactor.run()
```

Run the chat server with *python chatserver.py*. You can then connect to the chat server with the *telnet* utility. Example 2-6 shows a sample transcript of two users chatting.

Example 2-6. Using the chat server

```
$ telnet localhost 8000
Trying 127.0.0.1...
Connected to localhost.
Escape character is '^]'.
What's your name?
Jessica
Welcome, Jessica!
Adam has joined the channel.
Hey Adam!
<Adam> How's it going?
I've got a working Twisted chat server now, so pretty great!
^]
telnet> quit
Connection closed.

$ telnet localhost 8000
Trying 127.0.0.1...
Connected to localhost.
Escape character is '^]'.
What's your name?
Adam
Welcome, Adam!
<Jessica> Hey Adam!
How's it going?
<Jessica> I've got a working Twisted chat server now, so pretty great!
Jessica has left the channel.
```

 To terminate a *telnet* connection, hold down the Control key and press the right-bracket key. That will drop you to a `telnet>` prompt; from there, type `quit` and press the Return key to terminate the connection.

`ChatProtocol` has two states, `REGISTER` and `CHAT`. `lineReceived` calls the correct handler based on the current state of the protocol.

Note that the persistent protocol state—the dictionary of connected users—is stored in `ChatFactory`.

Avoid mixing application-specific logic with protocol code. This will make testing your protocol and application easier and facilitate protocol reuse.

As you can see, the servers and clients for the echo, quote, and chat services are all structurally very similar. The shared recipe is:

1. Define a protocol class, subclassing `twisted.internet.protocol.Protocol` for arbitrary data or `twisted.protocols.basic.LineReceiver` for line-oriented protocols.

2. Define a factory class, subclassing `twisted.internet.protocol.Factory` for servers and `twisted.internet.protocol.ClientFactory` for clients. That factory creates instances of the protocol and stores state shared across protocol instances.

3. Clients use `reactor.connectTCP` to initiate a connection to a server. Invoking `connectTCP` registers callbacks with the reactor to notify your protocol when new data has arrived across a socket for processing. Servers use `reactor.listenTCP` to listen for and respond to client connections.

4. Communication doesn't start until `reactor.run` is called, which starts the reactor event loop.

More Practice and Next Steps

This chapter introduced the core components of Twisted servers and clients: the reactor, transports, protocols, and protocol factories. Because a new instance of a protocol class is created for each connection, persistent state is kept in a protocol factory. Protocols and transports are decoupled, which makes transport reuse and protocol testing easy.

The Twisted Core examples directory (*http://bit.ly/XSAV56*) has many additional examples of basic servers and clients, including implementations for UDP and SSL.

The Twisted Core HOWTO index (*http://bit.ly/XSAXdq*) has an extended "Twisted from Scratch" tutorial that builds a `finger` service from scratch.

One real-world example of building a protocol in Twisted is AutobahnPython (*http:// bit.ly/XSAXdu*), a WebSockets implementation.

Twisted has been developing a new higher-level *endpoints API* for creating a connection between a client and server. The endpoints API wraps lower-level APIs like `listenTCP` and `connectTCP`, and provides greater flexibility because it decouples constructing a connection from initiating use of the connection, allowing parameterization of the endpoint. You'll start seeing the endpoints API in more documentation and examples through the next couple of Twisted releases, so keep an eye out for it. You can read more about that at the Twisted endpoints API page (*https://twistedmatrix.com/documents/current/core/howto/endpoints.html*).

CHAPTER 3

Writing Asynchronous Code with Deferreds

Callbacks are a fundamental part of event-driven programming and are the way that the reactor indicates to an application that an event has arrived. As event-driven programs grow, handling both the success and error cases for the events in one's application becomes increasingly complex. Failing to register an appropriate callback can leave a program blocking on event processing that will never happen, and errors might have to propagate up a chain of callbacks from the networking stack through the layers of an application.

Twisted provides an elegant abstraction called a Deferred to manage these callbacks. This chapter will give you practice using Deferreds by themselves and then demonstrate their real-world utility by integrating Deferreds into some client and server examples.

We'll use Deferreds while writing asynchronous servers and clients throughout the remainder of this book.

What Deferreds Do and Don't Do

It's worth heading off a common misconception up front:

- **Deferreds do help you write asynchronous code.**
- **Deferreds do not automatically make code asynchronous or nonblocking.** To turn a synchronous function into an asynchronous function, it'll need to be refactored to return a Deferred with which callbacks are registered.

Practice will help you develop an intuition for how to structure asynchronous code. Let's look at a Deferred so you can start getting some of that practice.

The Structure of a Deferred Object

Deferreds have a pair of callback chains, one for success (callbacks) and one for errors (errbacks). Deferreds start out with two empty chains. You add pairs of callbacks and errbacks to the Deferred to handle successes and failures at each point in the event processing. When an asynchronous result arrives, the Deferred is "fired" and the appropriate callbacks or errbacks are invoked in the order in which they were added to the chains. Figure 3-1 diagrams a Deferred and its callback chains.

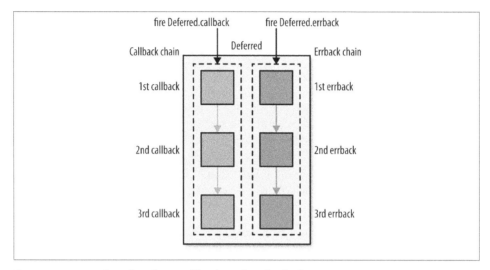

Figure 3-1. A Deferred with its callback and errback chains

To get a feel for how Deferreds work, we can create them, register callbacks and errbacks with them, and fire them without involving the reactor.

Example 3-1 creates a Deferred d and uses its addCallback method to register the function myCallback with the callback chain. d.callback "fires" d and invokes the callback chain, which only contains myCallback. The argument passed to callback is propagated as an argument to the first function in the callback chain.

Example 3-1. Using addCallback

```
from twisted.internet.defer import Deferred

def myCallback(result):
    print result

d = Deferred()
d.addCallback(myCallback)
d.callback("Triggering callback.")
```

Running Example 3-1 produces the following:

```
Triggering callback.
```

Example 3-2 creates a `Deferred` d and uses its `addErrback` method to register the function `myErrback` with the errback chain. `d.errback` "fires" d and invokes the first function in the errback chain, which only contains `myErrback`. The argument passed to `errback` is wrapped in a `Failure` object before getting passed to the errback function.

Example 3-2. Using addErrback

```
from twisted.internet.defer import Deferred

def myErrback(failure):
    print failure

d = Deferred()
d.addErrback(myErrback)
d.errback("Triggering errback.")
```

A `Failure` is Twisted's implementation of a dressed-up `Exception` suitable for asynchronous communication. It contains a stack trace for where an asynchronous error actually happened (which might not be the current stack trace).

Running Example 3-2 produces the following:

```
[Failure instance: Traceback (failure with no frames):
<class 'twisted.python.failure.DefaultException'>:
Triggering errback.
]
```

An asynchronous event may have many processing steps, each requiring a level of callbacks and errbacks. For example, a web request might need to be deserialized, formatted, and then cause a database insert, and each of those steps might possibly fail. `Deferreds` make it easy to manage these multiple levels of success and error handling in one place.

To register multiple levels of callbacks and errbacks with a `Deferred`, simply attach them to their callback chains in the order you want them invoked using `addCallback` and `addErrback`, as illustrated in Example 3-3. The result returned by a callback or errback in a `Deferred` chain is passed as the first argument to the next callback or errback in the chain.

Example 3-3. Registering multiple callbacks

```
from twisted.internet.defer import Deferred

def addBold(result):
    return "<b>%s</b>" % (result,)

def addItalic(result):
    return "<i>%s</i>" % (result,)
```

```
def printHTML(result):
    print result

d = Deferred()
d.addCallback(addBold)
d.addCallback(addItalic)
d.addCallback(printHTML)
d.callback("Hello World")
```

Running Example 3-3 produces:

```
<i><b>Hello World</b></i>
```

Note that registering a callback with `addCallback` also registers a "pass-through" for that level of the errback chain. Similarly, registering an errback with `addErrback` also registers a "pass-through" for that level of the callback chain. The chains always have the same length.

`Deferreds` also sport an `addCallbacks` method, which registers both a callback and an errback at the same level in their respective callback chains. For example:

```
d = Deferred()
d.addCallbacks(myCallback, myErrback)
d.callback("Triggering callback.")
```

Callback Chains and Using Deferreds in the Reactor

Now that we have experience playing with callbacks and errbacks outside the reactor, let's use them inside the reactor.

Example 3-4 retrieves a headline and then processes it, either converting it to HTML and then printing it or printing an error to *stderr* if the headline is too long.

Example 3-4. An asynchronous headline retriever

```
from twisted.internet import reactor, defer

class HeadlineRetriever(object):
    def processHeadline(self, headline):
        if len(headline) > 50:
            self.d.errback(
                "The headline ``%s'' is too long!" % (headline,))
        else:
            self.d.callback(headline)

    def _toHTML(self, result):
        return "<h1>%s</h1>" % (result,)

    def getHeadline(self, input):
        self.d = defer.Deferred()
        reactor.callLater(1, self.processHeadline, input)
        self.d.addCallback(self._toHTML)
```

```
        return self.d

def printData(result):
    print result
    reactor.stop()

def printError(failure):
    print failure
    reactor.stop()

h = HeadlineRetriever()
d = h.getHeadline("Breaking News: Twisted Takes Us to the Moon!")
d.addCallbacks(printData, printError)

reactor.run()
```

Running Example 3-4 produces:

```
<h1>Breaking News: Twisted Takes Us to the Moon!</h1>
```

Because the provided headline is fewer than 50 characters long, HeadlineRetriever fires the callback chain, invoking _toHTML and then printData, which prints the HTML headline.

Example 3-4 uses a helpful reactor method called callLater, which you can use to schedule events. In this example, we use callLater in getHeadline to fake an asynchronous event arriving after one second.

What happens when we replace the three lines before reactor.run() with the following?

```
h = HeadlineRetriever()
d = h.getHeadline("1234567890"*6)
d.addCallbacks(printData, printError)
```

Running this version of the example, we get:

```
[Failure instance: Traceback (failure with no frames):
<class 'twisted.python.failure.DefaultException'>:
The headline ``1234567890123456789<...>01234567890'' is too long!
]
```

In this version, HeadlineRetriever encounters a headline that is too long and fires the errback chain: a pass-through (from the call to addCallback(self._toHTML)), then printError. Figure 3-2 traces the path followed through the Deferred.

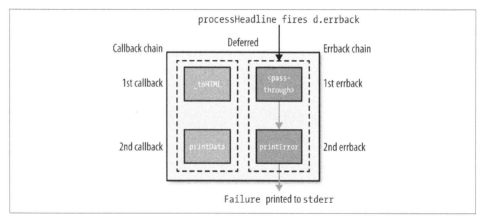

Figure 3-2. Error path through HeadlineRetriever's Deferred

Practice: What Do These Deferred Chains Do?

In this section, we'll look at a series of examples where the functions from Example 3-5 are chained together in various ways as callbacks and errbacks in a Deferred that is then fired. For each example, think about what sequence of callbacks and errbacks is executed and what the resulting output is. In examples where the output includes a traceback, the middle of the traceback has been elided for brevity and clarity.

Example 3-5. Various functions for use as callbacks and errbacks

```
from twisted.internet.defer import Deferred

def callback1(result):
    print "Callback 1 said:", result
    return result

def callback2(result):
    print "Callback 2 said:", result
    return result

def callback3(result):
    raise Exception("Callback 3")

def errback1(failure):
    print "Errback 1 had an an error on", failure
    return failure

def errback2(failure):
    raise Exception("Errback 2")

def errback3(failure):
    print "Errback 3 took care of", failure
    return "Everything is fine now."
```

Exercise 1

```
d = Deferred()
d.addCallback(callback1)
d.addCallback(callback2)
d.callback("Test")
```

When this Deferred fires, execution starts at the top of the callback chain; callback1 is executed, followed by callback2. The result is:

```
Callback 1 said: Test
Callback 2 said: Test
```

Exercise 2

```
d = Deferred()
d.addCallback(callback1)
d.addCallback(callback2)
d.addCallback(callback3)
d.callback("Test")
```

When this Deferred fires, execution starts at the top of the callback chain; callback1 is executed, followed by callback2, followed by callback3. callback3 raises an Exception, and because there is no registered errback to handle the Exception, the program terminates and reports an Unhandled Error to the user. The result is:

```
Callback 1 said: Test
Callback 2 said: Test
Unhandled error in Deferred:
Unhandled Error
Traceback (most recent call last):
  File "/tmp/test.py", line 33, in <module>
    d.callback("Test")
<...>
  File "/tmp/test.py", line 11, in callback3
    raise Exception("Callback 3")
exceptions.Exception: Callback 3
```

Exercise 3

```
d = Deferred()
d.addCallback(callback1)
d.addCallback(callback2)
d.addCallback(callback3)
d.addErrback(errback3)
d.callback("Test")
```

This Deferred has the same callbacks as the previous example, except that errback3 is also registered before firing. errback3 handles the Exception raised by callback3. The result is:

```
Callback 1 said: Test
Callback 2 said: Test
Errback 3 took care of [Failure instance:
Traceback: <type 'exceptions.Exception'>: Callback 3
test.py:40:<module>
<...>
test.py:11:callback3
```

Exercise 4

```
d = Deferred()
d.addErrback(errback1)
d.errback("Test")
```

This Deferred fires its errback chain. The first argument to an errback is always a Failure (being wrapped in one if necessary, as is the case with the "Test" string); errback1 returns the Failure, so that Failure is passed along as the argument to the next errback in the chain for processing. Because there is no additional errback to handle the Failure, execution stops with an Unhandled Error:

```
Errback 1 had an an error on [Failure instance:
Traceback (failure with no frames):
<class 'twisted.python.failure.DefaultException'>: Test
]
Unhandled error in Deferred:
Unhandled Error
Traceback (most recent call last):
Failure: twisted.python.failure.DefaultException: Test
```

Exercise 5

```
d = Deferred()
d.addErrback(errback1)
d.addErrback(errback3)
d.errback("Test")
```

This Deferred fires its errback chain, and errback1 propagates a Failure to errback3. errback3 handles the Failure by virtue of not raising an Exception or returning a Failure. It instead returns a string; because there is no callback at the next level to process the result, the Deferred is done firing.

```
Errback 1 had an an error on [Failure instance:
Traceback (failure with no frames):
<class 'twisted.python.failure.DefaultException'>: Test
]
Errback 3 took care of [Failure instance:
Traceback (failure with no frames):
<class 'twisted.python.failure.DefaultException'>: Test
]
```

Exercise 6

```
d = Deferred()
d.addErrback(errback2)
d.errback("Test")
```

This `Deferred` fires its errback chain, starting with `errback2`, which raises an `Exception`. Since raising an `Exception` passes control to the next errback in the chain, and there is no errback to handle the `Exception`, an `Unhandled Error` is raised:

```
Unhandled error in Deferred:
Unhandled Error
Traceback (most recent call last):
  File "test.py", line 59, in <module>
    d.errback("Test")
<...>
  File "test.py", line 18, in errback2
    raise Exception("Errback 2")
exceptions.Exception: Errback 2
```

The Truth About addCallbacks

Now that you have some `Deferred` practice under your belt, a somewhat subtle point needs to be made: `addCallbacks` is not the same as sequential calls to `addCallback` and `addErrback`.

What's the difference?

addCallbacks

> Registers a callback with the callback chain and an errback with the errback chain, *at the same level*

addCallback

> Registers a callback with the callback chain and a *pass-through* with the errback chain, which simply returns the result passed to it

addErrback

> Registers an errback with the errback chain and a pass-through with the callback chain

The salient difference is that callbacks and errbacks registered together using `addCallbacks` *do not interact*. Put another way, when a callback and an errback are registered together using `addCallbacks`, that errback can't handle exceptions raised by that callback: exceptions raised at level N in the callback chain are processed by the errback at level N + 1.

Figures 3-3 and 3-4 depict the difference between a call to `addCallbacks` and sequential calls to `addCallback` and `addErrback`.

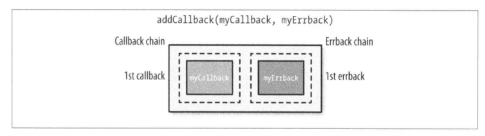

Figure 3-3. A single call to addCallbacks

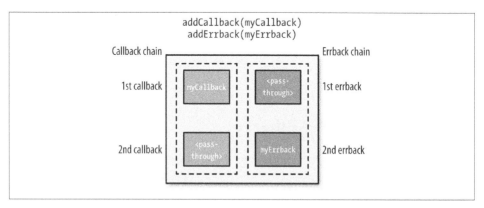

Figure 3-4. Sequential calls to addCallback and addErrback

Given this distinction, what do the following Deferred chains do?

Exercise 7

```
d = Deferred()
d.addCallback(callback1)
d.addCallback(callback2)
d.addCallbacks(callback3, errback3)
d.callback("Test")
```

This Deferred chain is the same as the one in Exercise 3, except that instead of calling addCallback(callback3) and addErrback(errback3) sequentially, they are registered together using addCallbacks. These code fragments *are not equivalent*! In Exercise 3, callback3 and a pass-through were registered as the callback and errback at level 3 for this Deferred, and then a pass-through and errback3 were registered as the callback and errback at level 4. This meant that an Exception raised on level 3 could be handled by the errback at level 4.

In Exercise 7, callback3 and errback3 are registered together as the callback and errback on level 3. This means there is no errback at level 4 to handle Exceptions raised at level 3. The result is:

```
Callback 1 said: Test
Callback 2 said: Test
Unhandled error in Deferred:
Unhandled Error
Traceback (most recent call last):
  File "test.py", line 46, in <module>
    d.callback("Test")
<...>
  File "test.py", line 11, in callback3
    raise Exception("Callback 3")
exceptions.Exception: Callback 3
```

Exercise 8

```
d = Deferred()
d.addCallback(callback3)
d.addCallbacks(callback2, errback3)
d.addCallbacks(callback1, errback2)
d.callback("Test")
```

This Deferred fires its callback chain. callback3 raises an Exception, so control passes to the next errback in the chain, errback3. errback3 handles the Exception, so control passes back to the callback chain and callback1 is invoked. The result is:

```
Errback 3 took care of [Failure instance:
Traceback: <type 'exceptions.Exception'>: Callback 3
test.py:75:<module>
<...>
test.py:11:callback3
]
Callback 1 said: Everything is fine now.
```

Key Facts About Deferreds

This section reiterates some important points about Deferreds and introduces a few new ones:

1. A Deferred is "fired" by invoking its callback or errback method.

2. A Deferred can only be fired once. Attempting to fire it again results in an AlreadyCalledError. This helps prevent accidentally processing an event more than once.

3. Exceptions at level N in the callback and errback chains are handled by the errback at level N + 1.

   If a callback or errback raises an Exception or returns a Failure at level N, the errback at level N + 1 is invoked to handle that error. If there is no errback, program execution stops and an Unhandled Error is reported.

If a callback or errback at level N *doesn't* raise an `Exception` or return a `Failure`, control is passed to the callback at level N + 1. Note that this applies to errbacks! If an errback doesn't produce an error, control passes to the callback chain. *Control will criss-cross between the errback and callback chains depending on the results of processing the event.*

4. The result returned by a callback in a `Deferred` chain is passed as the first argument to the next callback in the chain. This is what allows chaining processing of results. Don't forget to return the result from your callbacks for further processing!

5. If the object passed to an errback is not already a `Failure`, it is first wrapped in one. This includes objects passed to the errback chain when firing a `Deferred` and `Exceptions` raised by callbacks, which switch control to the errback chain for processing.

Summary of the Deferred API

The `Deferred` API has one last method for adding callbacks, `addBoth`, which adds the same callback to both the callback and errback chains for the `Deferred`. Note that while we haven't been passing arguments to our callback yet, that is supported by the API. The supported methods are:

addCallback
> Add a callback to the callback chain for the `Deferred` and add a pass-through to the errback chain.

addErrback
> Add an errback to the errback chain for the `Deferred` and add a pass-through to the callback chain. The analogous synchronous logic is the `except` part of a `try/except` block.

addCallbacks
> Add a callback and errback parallel to each other in the callback chains for the `Deferred`.

addBoth
> Add the same callback to both the callback and errback chains for the `Deferred`. The analogous synchronous logic is the `finally` part of a `try/except/finally` block.

More Practice and Next Steps

This chapter introduced the `Deferred`, an abstraction that simplifies and centralizes the management of callbacks for success and error handling in your asynchronous programs.

We'll use Deferreds while writing HTTP servers and clients in the next two chapters.

The Twisted Core HOWTO has two main documents on Deferreds, an overview (*http://bit.ly/XSAXtT*) of using them, and a guide (*http://bit.ly/XSAVlJ*) to writing functions that generate them.

CHAPTER 4

Web Servers

This chapter will first extend our experience with writing basic TCP servers to the construction of basic HTTP servers. With that context and understanding of the HTTP protocol in hand, we'll then abandon the low-level API in favor of the high-level `twisted.web` APIs used for constructing sophisticated web servers.

 Twisted Web is the Twisted subproject focusing on HTTP communication. It has robust HTTP 1.1 and HTTPS client and server implementations, proxy support, WSGI integration, basic HTML templating, and more.

Responding to HTTP Requests: A Low-Level Review

The HyperText Transfer Protocol (HTTP) is a request/response application-layer protocol, where requests are initiated by a client to a server, which responds with the requested resource. It is text-based and newline-delimited, and thus easy for humans to read.

To experiment with the HTTP protocol we'll create a subclass of `protocol.Protocol`, the same class we used to build our echo servers and clients in Chapter 2. Our protocol will know how to accept a connection, process the request, and send back an HTTP-formatted response.

This section is intended as both a glimpse under the hood and a refresher on the HTTP protocol. When building real web servers, you'll almost certainly use the higher-level `twisted.web` APIs Twisted provides. If you'd prefer to skip to that content, head over to "Handling GET Requests" on page 43.

The Structure of an HTTP Request

Every HTTP request starts with a single line containing the HTTP method, the path to the desired resource, and the HTTP version. Following this line are an arbitrary number of header lines. A blank line indicates the end of the headers. The header section is optionally followed by additional data called the *body* of the request, such as data being posted from an HTML form.

Here's an example of a minimal HTTP request. This request asks the server to perform the method GET on the root resource / using HTTP version 1.1:

```
GET / HTTP/1.1
Host: www.example.com
```

We can emulate a web browser and make this HTTP GET request manually using the *telnet* utility (taking care to remember the newline after the headers):

```
$ telnet www.google.com 80
Trying 74.125.131.99...
Connected to www.l.google.com.
Escape character is '^]'.
GET / HTTP/1.1
Host: www.google.com
```

The server responds with a line containing the HTTP version used for the response and an HTTP status code. Like the request, the response contains header lines followed by a blank line and the message body. A minimal HTTP response might look like this:

```
HTTP/1.1 200 OK
Content-Type: text/plain
Content-Length: 17
Connection: Close

Hello HTTP world!
```

www.google.com's response is more complicated, since it is setting cookies and various security headers, but the format is the same.

To write our own HTTP server, we can implement a Protocol that parses newline-delimited input, parses out the headers, and returns an HTTP-formatted response. Example 4-1 shows a simple HTTP implementation that echoes each request back to the client.

Example 4-1. webecho.py

```
from twisted.protocols import basic
from twisted.internet import protocol, reactor

class HTTPEchoProtocol(basic.LineReceiver):
    def __init__(self):
        self.lines = []
```

```
    def lineReceived(self, line):
        self.lines.append(line)
        if not line:
            self.sendResponse()

    def sendResponse(self):
        self.sendLine("HTTP/1.1 200 OK")
        self.sendLine("")
        responseBody = "You said:\r\n\r\n" + "\r\n".join(self.lines)
        self.transport.write(responseBody)
        self.transport.loseConnection()

class HTTPEchoFactory(protocol.ServerFactory):
    def buildProtocol(self, addr):
        return HTTPEchoProtocol()

reactor.listenTCP(8000, HTTPEchoFactory())
reactor.run()
```

As with our basic TCP servers from Chapter 2, we create a protocol factory, HTTPEchoFactory, inheriting from protocol.ServerFactory. It builds instances of our HTTPEchoProtocol, which inherits from basic.LineReceiver so we don't have to write our own boilerplate code for handling newline-delimited protocols.

We keep track of lines as they are received in lineReceived until we reach an empty line, the carriage return and line feed (\r\n) marking the end of the headers sent by the client. We then echo back the request text and terminate the connection.

HTTP uses TCP as its transport-layer protocol, so we use listenTCP to register callbacks with the reactor to get notified when TCP packets containing our HTTP data arrive on our designated port.

We can start this web server with *python webecho.py* then interact with the server through *telnet* or a web browser.

Using *telnet*, the communication will look something like:

```
$ telnet localhost 8000
Trying 127.0.0.1...
Connected to localhost.
Escape character is '^]'.
GET / HTTP/1.1
Host: localhost:8000
X-Header: "My test header"

HTTP/1.1 200 OK

You said:

GET / HTTP/1.1
Host: localhost:8000
```

```
X-Header: "My test header"
Connection closed by foreign host.
```

It's interesting to see what extra information your browser adds when making HTTP requests. To send a request to the server from a browser, visit *http://localhost:8000*.

Figure 4-1 shows what I get when I make this request from Chrome on my MacBook.

```
←    C    ⟳ localhost:8000                                          ☆  🖼  🔧

You said:

GET / HTTP/1.1
Host: localhost:8000
Connection: keep-alive
User-Agent: Mozilla/5.0 (Macintosh; Intel Mac OS X 10_6_8) AppleWebKit/536.5
(KHTML, like Gecko) Chrome/19.0.1084.56 Safari/536.5
Accept: text/html,application/xhtml+xml,application/xml;q=0.9,*/*;q=0.8
Accept-Encoding: gzip,deflate,sdch
Accept-Language: en-US,en;q=0.8
Accept-Charset: ISO-8859-1,utf-8;q=0.7,*;q=0.3
```

Figure 4-1. Browser GET request

By default, Chrome is telling websites about my operating system and browser and that I browse in English, as well as passing other headers specifying properties for the response.

Parsing HTTP Requests

The `HTTPEchoProtocol` class in Example 4-1 understands the structure of an HTTP request, but it doesn't know how to parse the request and respond with the resource being requested. To do this, we'll need to make our first foray into `twisted.web`.

An HTTP request is represented by `twisted.web.http.Request`. We can specify how requests are processed by subclassing `http.Request` and overriding its `process` method. Example 4-2 subclasses `http.Request` to serve one of three resources: an HTML page for the root resource /, a page for */about*, and a 404 `http.NOT_FOUND` if any other path is specified.

Example 4-2. requesthandler.py

```python
from twisted.internet import reactor
from twisted.web import http

class MyRequestHandler(http.Request):
    resources = {
        '/': '<h1>Home</h1>Home page',
        '/about': '<h1>About</h1>All about me',
        }
```

```
    def process(self):
        self.setHeader('Content-Type', 'text/html')
        if self.resources.has_key(self.path):
            self.write(self.resources[self.path])
        else:
            self.setResponseCode(http.NOT_FOUND)
            self.write("<h1>Not Found</h1>Sorry, no such resource.")
        self.finish()
class MyHTTP(http.HTTPChannel):
    requestFactory = MyRequestHandler

class MyHTTPFactory(http.HTTPFactory):
    def buildProtocol(self, addr):
        return MyHTTP()

reactor.listenTCP(8000, MyHTTPFactory())
reactor.run()
```

As always, we register a factory that generates instances of our protocol with the reactor. In this case, instead of subclassing protocol.Protocol directly, we are taking advantage of a higher-level API, http.HTTPChannel, which inherits from basic.LineReceiver and already understands the structure of an HTTP request and the numerous behaviors required by the HTTP RFCs.

Our MyHTTP protocol specifies how to process requests by setting its requestFactory instance variable to MyRequestHander, which subclasses http.Request. Request's process method is a noop that must be overridden in subclasses, which we do here. The HTTP response code is 200 unless overridden with setResponseCode, as we do to send a 404 http.NOT_FOUND when an unknown resource is requested.

To test this server, run *python requesthandler.py*; this will start up the web server on port 8000. You can then test accessing the supported resources, *http://localhost:8000/* and *http://localhost:8000/about*, and an unsupported resource like *http://localhost:8000/ foo*.

Handling GET Requests

Now that we have a good grasp of the structure of the HTTP protocol and how the low-level APIs work, we can move up to the high-level APIs in twisted.web.server that facilitate the construction of more sophisticated web servers.

Serving Static Content

A common task for a web server is to be able to serve static content out of some directory. Example 4-3 shows a basic implementation.

Example 4-3. static_content.py

```
from twisted.internet import reactor
from twisted.web.server import Site
from twisted.web.static import File

resource = File('/var/www/mysite')
factory = Site(resource)
reactor.listenTCP(8000, factory)
reactor.run()
```

At this level we no longer have to worry about HTTP protocol details. Instead, we use a Site, which subclasses http.HTTPFactory and manages HTTP sessions and dispatching to resources for us. A Site is initialized with the resource to which it is managing access.

A resource must provide the IResource interface, which describes how the resource gets rendered and how child resources in the resource hierarchy are added and accessed. In this case, we initialize our Site with a File resource representing a regular, noninterpreted file.

 twisted.web contains implementations for many common resources. Besides File, available resources include a customizable Directory Listing and ErrorPage, a ProxyResource that renders results retrieved from another server, and an XMLRPC implementation.

The Site is registered with the reactor, which will then listen for requests on port 8000.

After starting the web server with *python static_content.py*, we can visit *http://localhost: 8000* in a web browser. The server serves up a directory listing for all of the files in */var/ www/mysite/* (replace that path with a valid path to a directory on your system).

Static URL dispatch

What if you'd like to serve different content at different URLs?

We can create a hierarchy of resources to serve at different URLs by registering Resources as children of the root resource using its putChild method. Example 4-4 demonstrates this static URL dispatch.

Example 4-4. static_dispatch.py

```
from twisted.internet import reactor
from twisted.web.server import Site
from twisted.web.static import File

root = File('/var/www/mysite')
root.putChild("doc", File("/usr/share/doc"))
```

```
root.putChild("logs", File("/var/log/mysitelogs"))
factory = Site(root)
reactor.listenTCP(8000, factory)
reactor.run()
```

Now, visiting *http://localhost:8000/* in a web browser will serve content from */var/www/ mysite*, *http://localhost:8000/doc* will serve content from */usr/share/doc*, and *http:// localhost:8000/logs/* will serve content from */var/log/mysitelogs*.

These `Resource` hierarchies can be extended to arbitrary depths by registering child resources with existing resources in the hierarchy.

Serving Dynamic Content

Serving dynamic content looks very similar to serving static content—the big difference is that instead of using an existing `Resource`, like `File`, you'll subclass `Resource` to define the new dynamic resource you want a `Site` to serve.

Example 4-5 implements a simple clock page that displays the local time when you visit any URL.

Example 4-5. dynamic_content.py

```
from twisted.internet import reactor
from twisted.web.resource import Resource
from twisted.web.server import Site

import time

class ClockPage(Resource):
    isLeaf = True
    def render_GET(self, request):
        return "The local time is %s" % (time.ctime(),)

resource = ClockPage()
factory = Site(resource)
reactor.listenTCP(8000, factory)
reactor.run()
```

`ClockPage` is a subclass of `Resource`. We implement a `render_` method for every HTTP method we want to support; in this case we only care about supporting GET requests, so `render_GET` is all we implement. If we were to POST to this web server, we'd get a 405 Method Not Allowed unless we also implemented `render_POST`.

The rendering method is passed the request made by the client. This is not an instance of `twisted.web.http.Request`, as in Example 4-2; it is instead an instance of `twisted.web.server.Request`, which subclasses `http.Request` and understands application-layer ideas like session management and rendering.

render_GET returns whatever we want served as a response to a GET request. In this case, we return a string containing the local time. If we start our server with *python dynamic_content.py*, we can visit any URL on *http://localhost:8000* with a web browser and see the local time displayed and updated as we reload.

The isLeaf instance variable describes whether or not a resource will have children. Without more work on our part (as demonstrated in Example 4-6), only leaf resources get rendered; if we set isLeaf to False and restart the server, attempting to view any URL will produce a 404 No Such Resource.

Dynamic Dispatch

We know how to serve static and dynamic content. The next step is to be able to respond to requests dynamically, serving different resources based on the URL.

Example 4-6 demonstrates a calendar server that displays the calendar for the year provided in the URL. For example, visiting *http://localhost:8000/2013* will display the calendar for 2013, as shown in Figure 4-2.

Example 4-6. dynamic_dispatch.py

```python
from twisted.internet import reactor
from twisted.web.resource import Resource, NoResource
from twisted.web.server import Site

from calendar import calendar

class YearPage(Resource):
    def __init__(self, year):
        Resource.__init__(self)
        self.year = year

    def render_GET(self, request):
        return "<html><body><pre>%s</pre></body></html>" % (calendar(self.year),)

class CalendarHome(Resource):
    def getChild(self, name, request):
        if name == '':
            return self
        if name.isdigit():
            return YearPage(int(name))
        else:
            return NoResource()

    def render_GET(self, request):
        return "<html><body>Welcome to the calendar server!</body></html>"

root = CalendarHome()
factory = Site(root)
```

```
reactor.listenTCP(8000, factory)
reactor.run()
```

```
 ←  →  C   ☉ localhost:8000/2012

                                  2012

        January                  February                   March
  Mo Tu We Th Fr Sa Su      Mo Tu We Th Fr Sa Su      Mo Tu We Th Fr Sa Su
                    1                 1  2  3  4  5                    1  2  3  4
   2  3  4  5  6  7  8       6  7  8  9 10 11 12       5  6  7  8  9 10 11
   9 10 11 12 13 14 15      13 14 15 16 17 18 19      12 13 14 15 16 17 18
  16 17 18 19 20 21 22      20 21 22 23 24 25 26      19 20 21 22 23 24 25
  23 24 25 26 27 28 29      27 28 29                  26 27 28 29 30 31
  30 31
```

Figure 4-2. Calendar

This example has the same structure as Example 4-3. A TCP server is started on port 8000, serving the content registered with a Site, which is a subclass of twisted.web.http.HTTPFactory and knows how to manage access to resources.

The root resource is CalendarHome, which subclasses Resource to specify how to look up child resources and how to render itself.

CalendarHome.getChild describes how to traverse a URL from left to right until we get a renderable resource. If there is no additional component to the requested URL (i.e., the request was for /), CalendarHome returns itself to be rendered by invoking its render_GET method. If the URL has an additional component to its path that is an integer, an instance of YearPage is rendered. If that path component couldn't be converted to a number, an instance of twisted.web.error.NoResource is returned instead, which will render a generic 404 page.

There are a few subtle points to this example that deserve highlighting.

Creating resources that are both renderable and have children

Note that CalendarHome does not set isLeaf to True, and yet it is still rendered when we visit *http://localhost:8000*.

In general, only resources that are leaves are rendered; this can be because isLeaf is set to True or because when traversing the resource hierarchy, that resource is where we are when the URL runs out. However, when isLeaf is True for a resource, its getChild method is never called. Thus, for resources that have children, isLeaf cannot be set to True.

If we want CalendarHome to both get rendered and have children, we must override its getChild method to dictate resource generation.

In `CalendarHome.getChild`, if `name == ''` (i.e., if we are requesting the root resource), we return ourself to get rendered. Without that `if` condition, visiting *http://localhost: 8000* would produce a 404.

Similarly, `YearPage` does not have `isLeaf` set to `True`. That means that when we visit *http://localhost:8000/2013*, we get a rendered calendar because 2013 is at the end of the URL, but if we visit *http://localhost:8000/2013/foo*, we get a 404.

If we want *http://localhost:8000/2013/foo* to generate a calendar just like *http://localhost: 8000/2013*, we need to set `isLeaf` to `True` or have `YearPage` override `getChild` to return itself, like we do in `CalendarHome`.

Redirects

In Example 4-6, visiting *http://localhost:8000* produced a welcome page. What if we wanted *http://localhost:8000* to instead redirect to the calendar for the current year?

In the relevant render method (e.g., `render_GET`), instead of rendering the resource at a given URL, we need to construct a redirect with `twisted.web.util.redirectTo`. `redirectTo` takes as arguments the URL component to which to redirect, and the request, which still needs to be rendered.

Example 4-7 shows a revised `CalenderHome.render_GET` that redirects to the URL for the current year's calendar (e.g., *http://localhost:8000/2013*) upon requesting the root resource at *http://localhost:8000*.

Example 4-7. redirectTo

```
from datetime import datetime
from twisted.web.util import redirectTo

def render_GET(self, request):
    return redirectTo(datetime.now().year, request)
```

Handling POST Requests

To handle POST requests, implement a `render_POST` method in your `Resource`.

A Minimal POST Example

Example 4-8 serves a page where users can fill out and submit to the web server the contents of a text box. The server will then display that text back to the user.

Example 4-8. handle_post.py

```
from twisted.internet import reactor
from twisted.web.resource import Resource
from twisted.web.server import Site
```

```
import cgi

class FormPage(Resource):
    isLeaf = True
    def render_GET(self, request):
        return """
<html>
 <body>
  <form method="POST">
   <input name="form-field" type="text" />
   <input type="submit" />
   </form>
   </body>
   </html>
"""

    def render_POST(self, request):
        return """
<html>
 <body>You submitted: %s</body>
 </html>
""" % (cgi.escape(request.args["form-field"][0]),)

factory = Site(FormPage())
reactor.listenTCP(8000, factory)
reactor.run()
```

The FormPage Resource in *handle_post.py* implements both render_GET and render_POST methods.

render_GET returns the HTML for a blank page with a text box called "form-field". When a visitor visits *http://localhost:8000*, she will see this form.

render_POST extracts the text inputted by the user from request.args, sanitizes it with cgi.escape, and returns HTML displaying what the user submitted.

Asynchronous Responses

In all of the Twisted web server examples up to this point, we have assumed that the server can instantaneously respond to clients without having to first retrieve an expensive resource (say, from a database query) or do expensive computation. What happens when responding to a request blocks?

Example 4-9 implements a dummy BusyPage resource that sleeps for five seconds before returning a response to the request.

Example 4-9. blocking.py

```
from twisted.internet import reactor
from twisted.web.resource import Resource
```

```
from twisted.web.server import Site

import time

class BusyPage(Resource):
    isLeaf = True
    def render_GET(self, request):
        time.sleep(5)
        return "Finally done, at %s" % (time.asctime(),)


factory = Site(BusyPage())
reactor.listenTCP(8000, factory)
reactor.run()
```

If you run this server and then load *http://localhost:8000* in several browser tabs in quick succession, you'll observe that the last page to load will load N*5 seconds after the first page request, where N is the number of requests to the server. In other words, the requests are processed serially.

This is terrible performance! We need our web server to be responding to other requests while an expensive resource is being processed.

One of the great properties of this asynchronous framework is that we can achieve the responsiveness that we want without introducing threads by using the Deferred API we already know and love.

Example 4-10 demonstrates how to use a Deferred instead of blocking on an expensive resource. deferLater replaces the blocking time.sleep(5) with a Deferred that will fire after five seconds, with a callback to _delayedRender to finish the request when the fake resource becomes available. Then, instead of waiting on that resource, render_GET returns NOT_DONE_YET immediately, freeing up the web server to process other requests.

Example 4-10. non_blocking.py

```
from twisted.internet import reactor
from twisted.internet.task import deferLater
from twisted.web.resource import Resource
from twisted.web.server import Site, NOT_DONE_YET

import time

class BusyPage(Resource):
    isLeaf = True

    def _delayedRender(self, request):
        request.write("Finally done, at %s" % (time.asctime(),))
        request.finish()

    def render_GET(self, request):
        d = deferLater(reactor, 5, lambda: request)
```

```
        d.addCallback(self._delayedRender)
        return NOT_DONE_YET

factory = Site(BusyPage())
reactor.listenTCP(8000, factory)
reactor.run()
```

 If you run Example 4-10 and then load multiple instances of *http://
localhost:8000 in a browser, you may still find that the requests are processed serially. This is not Twisted's fault: some browsers, notably
Chrome, serialize requests to the same resource. You can verify that the
web server isn't blocking by issuing several simultaneous requests
through cURL or a quick Python script.

More Practice and Next Steps

This chapter introduced Twisted HTTP servers, from the lowest-level APIs up through
twisted.web.server. We saw examples of serving static and dynamic content, handling
GET and POST requests, and how to keep our servers responsive with asynchronous
responses using Deferreds.

The Twisted Web HOWTO index (*http://bit.ly/XSA VlP*) has several in-depth tutorials
related to HTTP servers, including on deployment and templating. This page (*http://
bit.ly/XSA Yhm*) is an excellent series of short, self-contained examples of Twisted Web
concepts.

The Twisted Web examples directory (*http://bit.ly/XSAZ4Z*) has a variety of server examples, including examples for proxies, an XML-RPC server, and rendering the output
of a server process.

Twisted is not a "web framework" like Django, web.py, or Flask. However, one of its
many roles is as a framework for building frameworks! An example of this is the Klein
micro-web framework (*http://bit.ly/XSAZBW*), which you can also browse and download at that GitHub page.

CHAPTER 5

Web Clients

This chapter will talk about the HTTP client side of Twisted Web, starting with quick web resource retrieval for one-off applications and ending with the `Agent` API for developing flexible web clients.

Basic HTTP Resource Retrieval

Twisted has several high-level convenience classes for quick one-off resource retrieval.

Printing a Web Resource

`twisted.web.client.getPage` asynchronously retrieves a resource at a given URL. It returns a `Deferred`, which fires its callback with the resource as a string. Example 5-1 demonstrates the use of `getPage`; it retrieves and prints the resource at the user-supplied URL.

Example 5-1. print_resource.py

```
from twisted.internet import reactor
from twisted.web.client import getPage
import sys

def printPage(result):
    print result

def printError(failure):
    print >>sys.stderr, failure

def stop(result):
    reactor.stop()

if len(sys.argv) != 2:
    print >>sys.stderr, "Usage: python print_resource.py <URL>"
    exit(1)
```

```
d = getPage(sys.argv[1])
d.addCallbacks(printPage, printError)
d.addBoth(stop)

reactor.run()
```

We can test this script with:

```
python print_resource.py http://www.google.com
```

which will print the contents of Google's home page to the screen.

An invalid URL will produce something like the following:

```
$ python print_resource.py http://notvalid.foo
[Failure instance: Traceback (failure with no frames):
<class 'twisted.internet.error.DNSLookupError'>:
DNS lookup failed: address 'notvalid.foo' not found:
[Errno 8] nodename nor servname provided, or not known.
]
```

Despite its name, getPage can make any HTTP request type. To make an HTTP POST request with getPage, supply the method and postdata keyword arguments: for example, getPage(sys.argv[1], method='POST', postdata="My test data").

getPage also supports using cookies, following redirects, and changing the User-Agent for the request.

Downloading a Web Resource

twisted.web.client.downloadPage asynchronously downloads a resource at a given URL to the specified file. Example 5-2 demonstrates the use of getPage.

Example 5-2. download_resource.py

```
from twisted.internet import reactor
from twisted.web.client import downloadPage
import sys

def printError(failure):
    print >>sys.stderr, failure

def stop(result):
    reactor.stop()

if len(sys.argv) != 3:
    print >>sys.stderr, "Usage: python download_resource.py <URL> <output file>"
    exit(1)

d = downloadPage(sys.argv[1], sys.argv[2])
d.addErrback(printError)
d.addBoth(stop)
```

```
reactor.run()
```

We can test this script with:

```
python download_resource.py http://www.google.com google.html
```

which will save the contents of Google's home page to the file *google.html*.

Agent

getPage and downloadPage are useful for getting small jobs done, but the main Twisted HTTP client API, which supports a broad range of RFC-compliant behaviors in a flexible and extensible way, is the Agent.

Requesting Resources with Agent

Example 5-3 implements the same functionality as print_resource.py from Example 5-1 using the Agent API.

Example 5-3. agent_print_resource.py

```
import sys

from twisted.internet import reactor
from twisted.internet.defer import Deferred
from twisted.internet.protocol import Protocol
from twisted.web.client import Agent

class ResourcePrinter(Protocol):
    def __init__(self, finished):
        self.finished = finished

    def dataReceived(self, data):
        print data

    def connectionLost(self, reason):
        self.finished.callback(None)

def printResource(response):
    finished = Deferred()
    response.deliverBody(ResourcePrinter(finished))
    return finished

def printError(failure):
    print >>sys.stderr, failure

def stop(result):
    reactor.stop()

if len(sys.argv) != 2:
```

```
    print >>sys.stderr, "Usage: python agent_print_resource.py URL"
    exit(1)

agent = Agent(reactor)
d = agent.request('GET', sys.argv[1])
d.addCallbacks(printResource, printError)
d.addBoth(stop)

reactor.run()
```

The agent version requires a bit more work but is much more general-purpose. Let's break down the steps involved:

1. Initialize an instance of `twisted.web.client.Agent`. Because the agent handles connection setup, it must be initialized with a reactor.

2. Make an HTTP request with the agent's `request` method. It takes at minimum the HTTP method and URL. On success, `agent.request` returns a `Deferred` that fires with a `Response` object encapsulating the response to the request.

3. Register a callback with the `Deferred` returned by `agent.request` to handle the `Response` body as it becomes available through `response.deliverBody`. Because the response is coming across the network in chunks, we need a `Protocol` that will process the data as it is received and notify us when the body has been completely delivered.

   To accomplish this, we create a `Protocol` subclass called `ResourcePrinter`, similar to how we did when constructing basic TCP servers and clients in Chapter 2. The big difference is that we want to be able to continue processing the event outside of `ResourcePrinter`. That link to the outside world will be a `Deferred` that is passed to a `ResourcePrinter` instance on initialization and is fired when the connection has been terminated. That `Deferred` is created and returned by `printResource` so more callbacks can be registered for additional processing. As chunks of the response body arrive, the reactor invokes `dataReceived`, and we print the data to the screen. When the reactor invokes `connectionLost`, we trigger the `Deferred`.

4. Once the connection has been terminated, stop the reactor. To do this, we register callbacks to a `stop` function with the `Deferred` triggered by `connectionLost` and returned by `printResource`. Recall that `addBoth` registers the same function with both the callback and errback chains, so the reactor will be stopped whether or not the download was successful.

5. Finally, run the reactor, which will kick off the HTTP request.

Running this example with *python agent_print_resource.py http://www.google.com* produces the same output as Example 5-1.

Retrieving Response Metadata

Agent supports all HTTP methods and arbitrary HTTP headers. Example 5-4 demonstrates this functionality with an HTTP HEAD request.

The Response object in the Deferred returned by agent.request contains lots of useful HTTP response metadata, including the HTTP status code, HTTP version, and headers. Example 5-4 also demonstrates extracting this information.

Example 5-4. print_metadata.py

```
import sys

from twisted.internet import reactor
from twisted.web.client import Agent
from twisted.web.http_headers import Headers

def printHeaders(response):
    print 'HTTP version:', response.version
    print 'Status code:', response.code
    print 'Status phrase:', response.phrase
    print 'Response headers:'
    for header, value in response.headers.getAllRawHeaders():
        print header, value

def printError(failure):
    print >>sys.stderr, failure

def stop(result):
    reactor.stop()

if len(sys.argv) != 2:
    print >>sys.stderr, "Usage: python print_metadata.py URL"
    exit(1)

agent = Agent(reactor)
headers = Headers({'User-Agent': ['Twisted WebBot'],
                   'Content-Type': ['text/x-greeting']})

d = agent.request('HEAD', sys.argv[1], headers=headers)
d.addCallbacks(printHeaders, printError)
d.addBoth(stop)

reactor.run()
```

Testing this script with a URL like:

```
python print_metadata.py http://www.google.com/
```

produces the following output:

```
HTTP version: ('HTTP', 1, 1)
Status code: 200
```

```
Status phrase: OK
Response headers:
X-Xss-Protection ['1; mode=block']
Set-Cookie ['PREF=ID=b1401ec53122a4e5:FF=0:TM=1340750440...
Expires ['-1']
Server ['gws']
Cache-Control ['private, max-age=0']
Date ['Tue, 26 Jun 2012 22:40:40 GMT']
P3p ['CP="This is not a P3P policy! See http://www.google.com/support/...
Content-Type ['text/html; charset=ISO-8859-1']
X-Frame-Options ['SAMEORIGIN']
```

POSTing Data with Agent

To POST HTTP data with Agent, we need to construct a producer, providing the IBo dyProducer interface, which will produce the POST data when the Agent needs it.

 The producer/consumer design pattern facilitates streaming potentially large amounts of data in a way that is memory- and CPU-efficient even if processes are producing and consuming at different rates.

You can also read more about Twisted's producer/consumer APIs (*http://bit.ly/XSB2h7*).

To provide the IBodyProducer interface, which is enforced by Twisted's use of zope.interface.implements, a class must implement the following methods, as well as a length attribute tracking the length of the data the producer will eventually produce:

- startProducing
- stopProducing
- pauseProducing
- resumeProducing

For this example, we can construct a simple StringProducer that just writes out the POST data to the waiting consumer when startProducing is invoked. StringProducer is passed as the bodyProducer argument to agent.request.

Example 5-5 shows a complete POSTing client. Beyond the StringProducer, the code is almost identical to the resource-requesting client in Example 5-3.

Example 5-5. post_data.py

```
import sys
from twisted.internet import reactor
from twisted.internet.defer import Deferred, succeed
from twisted.internet.protocol import Protocol
```

```python
from twisted.web.client import Agent
from twisted.web.iweb import IBodyProducer

from zope.interface import implements

class StringProducer(object):
    implements(IBodyProducer)

    def __init__(self, body):
        self.body = body
        self.length = len(body)

    def startProducing(self, consumer):
        consumer.write(self.body)
        return succeed(None)

    def pauseProducing(self):
        pass

    def stopProducing(self):
        pass

    class ResourcePrinter(Protocol):
        def __init__(self, finished):
            self.finished = finished

        def dataReceived(self, data):
            print data

        def connectionLost(self, reason):
            self.finished.callback(None)

    def printResource(response):
        finished = Deferred()
        response.deliverBody(ResourcePrinter(finished))
        return finished

    def printError(failure):
        print >>sys.stderr, failure

    def stop(result):
        reactor.stop()

    if len(sys.argv) != 3:
        print >>sys.stderr, "Usage: python post_resource.py URL 'POST DATA'"
        exit(1)

    agent = Agent(reactor)
    body = StringProducer(sys.argv[2])
    d = agent.request('POST', sys.argv[1], bodyProducer=body)
    d.addCallbacks(printResource, printError)
    d.addBoth(stop)
```

```
    reactor.run()
```

To test this example, we need a URL that accepts POST requests. *http:// www.google.com* is not such a URL, as it turns out. This:

```
python post_data.py http://www.google.com 'Hello World'
```

prints:

```
The request method POST is inappropriate for the URL /. That's all we know.
```

This is an occasion where being able to spin up a basic web server easily for testing would be useful. Fortunately, we covered Twisted web servers in the previous chapter!

Example 5-6 is a simple web server that echoes the body of a POST, only reversed.

Example 5-6. test_server.py

```python
from twisted.internet import reactor
from twisted.web.resource import Resource
from twisted.web.server import Site

class TestPage(Resource):
    isLeaf = True
    def render_POST(self, request):
        return request.content.read()[::-1]

resource = TestPage()
factory = Site(resource)
reactor.listenTCP(8000, factory)
reactor.run()
```

python test_server.py will start the web server listening on port 8000. With that server running, we can then test our client with:

```
$ python post_data.py http://127.0.0.1:8000 'Hello World'
dlroW olleH
```

More Practice and Next Steps

This chapter introduced Twisted HTTP clients. High-level helpers `getPage` and `downloadPage` make quick resource retrieval easy. The `Agent` is a flexible and comprehensive API for writing web clients.

The Twisted Web Client HOWTO (*http://bit.ly/XSB2hl*) discusses the `Agent` API in detail, including handling proxies and cookies.

The Twisted Web examples directory (*http://bit.ly/XSAZ4Z*) has a variety of HTTP client examples.

PART II

Building Production-Grade
Twisted Services

CHAPTER 6

Deploying Twisted Applications

Twisted is an engine for producing scalable, cross-platform network servers and clients. Making it easy to deploy these applications in a standardized fashion in production environments is an important part of a platform like this getting wide-scale adoption.

To that end, Twisted provides an application infrastructure: a reusable and configurable way to deploy a Twisted application. It allows a programmer to avoid boilerplate code by hooking an application into existing tools for customizing the way it is run, including daemonization, logging, using a custom reactor, profiling code, and more.

The Twisted Application Infrastructure

The application infrastructure has five main components: services, applications, TAC files, plugins, and the *twistd* command-line utility. To illustrate this infrastructure, we'll turn the echo server from Chapter 2 into an application. Example 6-1 reproduces the server code.

Example 6-1. echoserver.py from Chapter 2

```
from twisted.internet import protocol, reactor

class Echo(protocol.Protocol):
    def dataReceived(self, data):
        self.transport.write(data)

class EchoFactory(protocol.Factory):
    def buildProtocol(self, addr):
        return Echo()

reactor.listenTCP(8000, EchoFactory())
reactor.run()
```

Services

A service is anything that can be started and stopped and that implements the `IService` interface. Twisted comes with service implementations for TCP, FTP, HTTP, SSH, DNS, and many other protocols. Many services can register with a single application.

The core of the `IService` interface is:

`startService`
> Start the service. This might include loading configuration data, setting up database connections, or listening on a port.

`stopService`
> Shut down the service. This might include saving state to disk, closing database connections, or stopping listening on a port.

Our echo service uses TCP, so we can use Twisted's default `TCPServer` implementation of this `IService` interface.

Applications

An application is the top-level container for one or more services that are deployed together. Services register themselves with an application, and the *twistd* deployment utility described shortly searches for and runs applications.

We'll create an echo application with which the echo service can register.

TAC Files

When writing a Twisted program as a regular Python file, the developer is responsible for writing code to start and stop the reactor and to configure the program. Under the Twisted application infrastructure, protocol implementations live in a module, services using those protocols are registered in a Twisted application configuration (TAC) file, and the reactor and configuration are managed by an external utility.

To turn our echo server into an echo application, we can follow a simple algorithm:

1. Move the `Protocol` and `Factory` for the service into their own module.
2. Inside a TAC file:
   a. Create an instance of `twisted.application.service.Application`.
   b. Instead of registering the `Protocol Factory` with a reactor, like in Chapter 2, register the factory with a service, and register that service with the `Application`.

In our case, this means creating an instance of the `TCPServer` service, which will use our `EchoFactory` to create instances of the `Echo` protocol on port 8000.

The code for managing the reactor will be taken care of by *twistd*, which we'll discuss next. The application code is now split into two files: *echo.py*, shown in Example 6-2; and *echo_server.tac*, shown in Example 6-3.

Example 6-2. echo.py, a module containing the Protocol and Factory definitions

```
from twisted.internet import protocol, reactor

class Echo(protocol.Protocol):
    def dataReceived(self, data):
        self.transport.write(data)

class EchoFactory(protocol.Factory):
    def buildProtocol(self, addr):
        return Echo()
```

Example 6-3. echo_server.tac, a Twisted application configuration file

```
from twisted.application import internet, service
from echo import EchoFactory

application = service.Application("echo")
echoService = internet.TCPServer(8000, EchoFactory())
echoService.setServiceParent(application)
```

twistd

twistd (pronounced "twist-dee") is a cross-platform utility for deploying Twisted applications. It runs TAC files and handles starting and stopping the application. As part of Twisted's batteries-included approach to network programming, *twistd* comes with a number of useful configuration flags, including flags for daemonizing the application, specifying the location of log files, dropping privileges, running in a chroot, running under a non-default reactor, or even running the application under a profiler.

We can run our echo server application with:

```
twistd -y echo_server.tac
```

In this simplest case, *twistd* starts a daemonized instance of the application, logging to *twistd.log*, with a PID stored in *twisted.pid*. After starting and stopping the application, the log looks like this:

```
2012-11-19 22:23:07-0500 [-] Log opened.
2012-11-19 22:23:07-0500 [-] twistd 12.1.0 (/usr/bin/python 2.7.1) ...
2012-11-19 22:23:07-0500 [-] reactor class: twisted.internet.select...
2012-11-19 22:23:07-0500 [-] echo.EchoFactory starting on 8000
2012-11-19 22:23:07-0500 [-] Starting factory <echo.EchoFactory ...
2012-11-19 22:23:20-0500 [-] Received SIGTERM, shutting down.
2012-11-19 22:23:20-0500 [-] (TCP Port 8000 Closed)
2012-11-19 22:23:20-0500 [-] Stopping factory <echo.EchoFactory ...
```

```
2012-11-19 22:23:20-0500 [-] Main loop terminated.
2012-11-19 22:23:20-0500 [-] Server Shut Down.
```

To suppress daemonization and log to *stdout*, pass *-n* (*--nodaemon*). For a full list of *twistd*'s capabilities, run *twistd --help* or consult the manpage.

Without writing any code ourselves, we got free daemonization and logging. Running a service using the Twisted application infrastructure allows developers to skip writing boilerplate code for common server functionalities.

Plugins

An alternative to the TAC-based system for running Twisted applications is the plugin system. While the TAC system makes it easy to register simple hierarchies of predefined services within an application configuration file, the plugin system makes it easy to register custom services as subcommands of the *twistd* utility and to extend the command-line interface to an application.

Using this system:

- Only the plugin API is required to remain stable, which makes it easy for third-party developers to extend the software.
- Plugin discoverability is codified. Plugins can be loaded and saved when a program is first run, rediscovered each time the program starts up, or polled for repeatedly at runtime, allowing the discovery of new plugins installed after the program has started.

To extend a program using the Twisted plugin system, all you have to do is create objects that implement the IPlugin interface and put them in a particular location where the plugin system knows to look for them.

Having already converted our echo server to a Twisted application, transformation into a Twisted plugin is straightforward. Alongside the echo module from before, which contains the Echo protocol and EchoFactory definitions, we add a directory called *twisted*, containing a subdirectory called *plugins* containing our echo plugin definition. Graphically, the directory structure is:

```
echoproject/
├── echo.py
└── twisted
    └── plugins
        └── echo_plugin.py
```

Let's make the port our echo service uses configurable through *twistd*. Example 6-4 shows the necessary logic.

Example 6-4. echo_plugin.py

```python
from zope.interface import implements

from twisted.application.service import IServiceMaker
from twisted.application import internet
from twisted.plugin import IPlugin
from twisted.python import usage

from echo import EchoFactory

class Options(usage.Options):
    optParameters = [["port", "p", 8000, "The port number to listen on."]]

class EchoServiceMaker(object):
    implements(IServiceMaker, IPlugin)
    tapname = "echo"
    description = "A TCP-based echo server."
    options = Options

    def makeService(self, options):
        """
        Construct a TCPServer from a factory defined in echo.py.
        """
        return internet.TCPServer(int(options["port"]), EchoFactory())

serviceMaker = EchoServiceMaker()
```

A service plugin needs a minimum of two components:

1. A subclass of `twisted.python.usage.Options`, with a class variable `optParameters` describing each of the command-line options to the service.

    In our case, `optParameters` describes a single *-p/--port* configuration option, which has a default of 8000.

2. An implementor of both `IPlugin` and `IServiceMaker`. This class implements a `makeService` method that passes the command-line configuration options to the service. It also defines the name and description of the service as displayed by *twistd*.

    In our case, as with the TAC implementation, we'll create instances of the `TCPServer` service, but with a port pulled from the command-line options instead of hard-coding 8000.

With this plugin defined, if we run *twistd* from the top-level project directory our echo server will now show up as a server option in the output of *twistd --help*, and running *twistd echo --port=1235* will start an echo server on port 1235.

More twistd Examples

twistd ships with many commands that make it easy to spin up simple services with zero lines of code. Here are some examples:

twistd web --port 8080 --path .

> Run an HTTP server on port 8080, serving both static and dynamic content out of the current working directory. Visit *http://localhost:8080* to see the directory listing.

twistd dns -v -p 5553 --hosts-file=hosts

> Run a DNS server on port 5553, resolving domains out of a file called *hosts* in the format of */etc/hosts*.
>
> For example, say you'd like to run your own Twisted DNS resolver and are also trying to cut back on social media. Create a *hosts* file that resolves *facebook.com*, *twitter.com*, and *reddit.com* to *localhost*, 127.0.0.1:

```
127.0.0.1 facebook.com
127.0.0.1 twitter.com
127.0.0.1 reddit.com
```

> Then run your *twistd* DNS resolver, configure your operating system to try that resolver first, and effectively disable your ability to view those sites.
>
> A quick command-line way to prove that the resolver is working is to use the *dig* DNS lookup utility. First, query the default resolver, then query the *twistd* resolver:

```
$ dig +short twitter.com
199.59.150.7
199.59.148.10
199.59.150.39
$ dig @localhost -p 5553 +short twitter.com
127.0.0.1
```

sudo twistd conch -p tcp:2222

> Run an *ssh* server on port 2222. *ssh* keys must be set up independently.

twistd mail -E -H localhost -d localhost=emails

> Run an ESMTP POP3 server, accepting email for *localhost* and saving it to the *emails* directory.

I don't know about you, but I get pretty excited by the networking power of these simple *twistd* one-liners.

More Practice and Next Steps

This chapter introduced the Twisted application infrastructure for configuring and deploying Twisted programs in a standardized fashion.

There are two main ways of deploying applications using this infrastructure: TAC files and plugins. TAC files are simpler but less extensible, making them ideal for simple server deployments that want to take advantage of Twisted's built-in deployment features, like logging and daemonization. Plugins have a higher initial development cost but expose a clear API for extending your application. Plugins are ideal for applications that need a stable interface for third-party developers or more control over plugin discovery and loading.

The Twisted Core HOWTO provides an overview of the application framework (*http://bit.ly/XSB0pr*) and TAC files, as well as information about the plugin philosophy (*http://bit.ly/XSB2O7*) and *twistd* plugins (*http://bit.ly/XSB2Od*) specifically.

Twisted comes with a pluggable authentication system for servers called Twisted Cred, and a common use of the plugin system is to add authentication to an application. Twisted Cred is discussed in detail in Chapter 9.

Suggested Exercises

1. Converting a Twisted program into a TAC-based or plugin-based service follows a straightforward algorithm that you can practice on any of the servers we build in this book.

   Try converting the chat server from Example 2-5 to a Twisted application, and converting the nonblocking web server from Example 4-8 to a plugin-based service.

2. All of the commands listed in *twistd --help* are plugins that you can browse in the Twisted source code at *twisted/plugins/*. Pick one and read through the service definition.

CHAPTER 7

Logging

Twisted has its own logging systems that we've already seen used under the hood by *twistd*. This system plays nicely with Twisted-specific concepts like Failures but is also compatible with Python's standard library logging facilities.

Basic In-Application Logging

The simplest way to add logging to your Twisted application is to import twisted.python.log, start logging to a file or *stdout*, and log events at particular log levels as you would with the Python standard logging module. For instance, Example 7-1 adds logging to a file for our echo server from Chapter 2.

Example 7-1. logging_echoserver.py

```
from twisted.internet import protocol, reactor
from twisted.python import log

class Echo(protocol.Protocol):
    def dataReceived(self, data):
        log.msg(data)
        self.transport.write(data)

class EchoFactory(protocol.Factory):
    def buildProtocol(self, addr):
        return Echo()

log.startLogging(open('echo.log', 'w'))
reactor.listenTCP(8000, EchoFactory())
reactor.run()
```

Logging starts once log.startLogging has been called. After that, information can be logged with log.msg or log.err; use log.msg to log strings and use log.err to log exceptions and failures. The default logging format produces output like this log of the echo server starting up, echoing one message, and terminating:

```
2012-11-15 20:26:37-0500 [-] Log opened.
2012-11-15 20:26:37-0500 [-] EchoFactory starting on 8000
2012-11-15 20:26:37-0500 [-] Starting factory <__main__.EchoFactory ...
2012-11-15 20:26:40-0500 [Echo,0,127.0.0.1] Hello, world!
2012-11-15 20:26:43-0500 [-] Received SIGINT, shutting down.
2012-11-15 20:26:43-0500 [__main__.EchoFactory] (TCP Port 8000 Closed)
2012-11-15 20:26:43-0500 [__main__.EchoFactory] Stopping factory <__...
2012-11-15 20:26:43-0500 [-] Main loop terminated.
```

To log to *stdout*, call `startLogging` with `sys.stdout`, as in Example 7-2.

Example 7-2. logging_test.py

```python
import sys
from twisted.python import log

log.startLogging(sys.stdout)
log.msg("Starting experiment")

log.msg("Logging an exception")

try:
    1 / 0
except ZeroDivisionError, e:
    log.err(e)

log.msg("Ending experiment")
```

By default, in addition to logging messages when you invoke `log.msg` and `log.err`, the logging facilities will log *stdout* (e.g., print statements) as well as tracebacks for uncaught `exceptions`. They will also listen for and log events emitted by Twisted modules. That's why we see various `EchoFactory` events in the preceding logs.

Twisted has some convenience classes for customizing your log file management. One example is `twisted.python.logfile.LogFile`, which can be rotated manually or when a specified log size has been reached. Example 7-3 illustrates both features.

Example 7-3. log_rotation.py

```python
from twisted.python import log
from twisted.python import logfile

# Log to /tmp/test.log ... test.log.N, rotating every 100 bytes.
f = logfile.LogFile("test.log", "/tmp", rotateLength=100)
log.startLogging(f)

log.msg("First message")

# Rotate manually.
```

```
f.rotate()

for i in range(5):
    log.msg("Test message", i)

log.msg("Last message")
```

As *log_rotation.py* runs, messages will be logged to */tmp/test.log*. When the logs are rotated manually or `rotateLength` is met, the existing log numbers are incremented (e.g., */tmp/test.log.1* becomes */tmp/test.log.2*, and */tmp/test.log* becomes */tmp/test.log.1*) and a fresh */tmp/test.log* is produced. By the end, "First message" is in the oldest log, */tmp/test.log.2*, and "Last message" is in */tmp/test.log*.

Since daily log rotation is such a common action, Twisted also has a `DailyLogFile` class that will auto-rotate logs each day.

twistd Logging

As we saw in Chapter 6, Twisted applications run with *twistd* utilize Twisted's logging by default, printing to *twistd.log* if daemonized or to *stdout* if not.

twistd's built-in logging can be customized through command-line arguments: specify a log file with *--logfile* (use - for *stdout*) and pass *--syslog* to log to *syslog* instead of a log file.

For further customization of logging, including changing the log prefix (by default, a timestamp like `2012-08-20 22:08:34-0400`), we'll need to implement our own `LogObserver`.

Custom Loggers

As an example, what if we wanted a logger that logged to *stdout* and colored error messages red? Example 7-4 demonstrates how to subclass `FileLogObserver` and override the `emit` method to achieve this.

Example 7-4. log_colorizer.py

```
import sys

from twisted.python.log import FileLogObserver

class ColorizedLogObserver(FileLogObserver):
    def emit(self, eventDict):
        # Reset text color.
        self.write("\033[0m")

        if eventDict["isError"]:
            # ANSI escape sequence to color text red.
```

```
        self.write("\033[91m")

    FileLogObserver.emit(self, eventDict)

def logger():
    return ColorizedLogObserver(sys.stdout).emit
```

`FileLogObserver.emit` is an observer. Whenever `log.msg` or `log.err` is called, observers registered through `log.addObserver` receive that event. You can register as many observers as you want, so a single event can be processed in many ways.

`startLogging` and *twistd* call `log.addObserver` under the hood. As an example of registering your own observer, we can add `ColorizedLogObserver`'s colorized alert logging to our logging test from Example 7-2, as shown in Example 7-5.

Example 7-5. colorized_logging_test.py

```
import sys
from twisted.python import log
from log_colorizer import ColorizedLogObserver

observer = ColorizedLogObserver(sys.stdout)
log.addObserver(observer.emit)

log.msg("Starting experiment")

log.msg("Logging an exception")

try:
    1 / 0
except ZeroDivisionError, e:
    log.err(e)

log.msg("Ending experiment")
```

The only change we had to make to use our custom logger was registering an instance of `ColorizedLogObserver` with `log.addObserver`.

We can also use `ColorizedLogObserver` as a custom logger for *twistd* programs by passing a log observer factory (i.e., the `emit` method of an instance of a `LogObserver`) through the *--logger* command-line option. For example, to run our *echo_server.tac* from Chapter 6 with colorized logging to *stdout*, we could use this command line:

```
twistd -ny echo_server.tac --logger=log_colorizer.logger --logfile=-
```

The hyphen at the end of *--logfile=-* specifies logging to *stdout*. *-n* says don't daemonize.

Key Facts and Caveats About Logging

Here are some things to keep in mind regarding logging in Twisted:

- Use `log.startLogging` to start logging to a file, either directly or through a convenience class like `DailyLogFile`.
- Events are logged with `log.msg` and `log.err`. By default, `log.startLogging` will also redirect *stdout* and *stderr* to the log.
- Use `log.addObserver` to register custom loggers.
- When you are writing custom log observers, never block, or your whole event loop will block. The observer must also be thread-safe if it is going to be used in multi-threaded programs.
- Applications run with *twistd* have logging enabled automatically. Logging can be customized through *--logfile*, *--syslog*, and *--logger*.

CHAPTER 8

Databases

Because Twisted applications run in an event loop, the application must not make blocking calls in the main thread or the entire event loop will stall. Because most databases expose a blocking API, Twisted provides `twisted.enterprise.adbapi` as a non-blocking interface to the DB-API 2.0 API implemented by Python bindings for most popular databases, including MySQL, Postgres, and SQLite.

Nonblocking Database Queries

Switching from the blocking API to `adbapi` is a straightforward transformation: instead of creating individual database connections, use a connection from `adbapi.ConnectionPool`, which manages a pool of connections run in separate threads for you. Once you have a database cursor, instead of using the blocking `execute` and `fetchall` methods, use `dbpool.runQuery` to execute a SQL query and return the result.

Example 8-1 demonstrates executing a nonblocking SELECT query on a hypothetical SQLite database called *users.db* (the errback has been omitted for brevity).

Example 8-1. db_test.py

```
from twisted.internet import reactor
from twisted.enterprise import adbapi

dbpool = adbapi.ConnectionPool("sqlite3", "users.db")

def getName(email):
    return dbpool.runQuery("SELECT name FROM users WHERE email = ?",
                           (email,))

def printResults(results):
    for elt in results:
        print elt[0]
```

```
def finish():
    dbpool.close()
    reactor.stop()

d = getName("jane@foo.com")
d.addCallback(printResults)

reactor.callLater(1, finish)
reactor.run()
```

 When using adbapi with SQLite, if you encounter an error of the form:

```
sqlite3.ProgrammingError: SQLite objects created in a thread
can only be used in that same thread.The object was created in
thread id 5972 and this is thread id 4916
```

you'll need to create your ConnectionPool with check_same_thread=False, as in:

```
dbpool = adbapi.ConnectionPool("sqlite3", "users.db",
                               check_same_thread=False)
```

See Twisted ticket 3629 (*http://bit.ly/XSB34H*) for details.

The first argument to adbapi.ConnectPool is the import string for the desired database bindings. The rest of the arguments are passed to the underlying connect method for your database bindings and thus differ based on which database you are using. For example, connecting to a MySQL database might look like adbapi.Connec tionPool("MySQLdb", db="users").

dbpool.runQuery returns a Deferred, so we can attach callbacks and errbacks for processing the result of the query just as we've done with Deferreds in previous chapters.

The parts of the API you are most likely to use map neatly to blocking counterparts:

adbapi.ConnectionPool()
    connection = *db-module*.connect() followed by cursor = connection. cursor()

runOperation()
    cursor.execute()

runQuery()
    cursor.execute() followed by cursor.fetchall()

runInteraction()
    Running multiple queries inside a transaction

Note that because we are using a ConnectionPool, we don't have to take care of connecting to or disconnecting from the database.

Example 8-2 uses `runInteraction` to create the SQLite users database from Example 8-1.

Example 8-2. db_transaction_test.py

```
from twisted.internet import reactor
from twisted.enterprise import adbapi

dbpool = adbapi.ConnectionPool("sqlite3", "users.db")

def _createUsersTable(transaction, users):
    transaction.execute("CREATE TABLE users (email TEXT, name TEXT)")
    for email, name in users:
        transaction.execute("INSERT INTO users (email, name) VALUES(?, ?)",
                            (email, name))

def createUsersTable(users):
    return dbpool.runInteraction(_createUsersTable, users)

def getName(email):
    return dbpool.runQuery("SELECT name FROM users WHERE email = ?",
                            (email,))

def printResults(results):
    for elt in results:
        print elt[0]

def finish():
    dbpool.close()
    reactor.stop()

users = [("jane@foo.com", "Jane"), ("joel@foo.com", "Joel")]
d = createUsersTable(users)
d.addCallback(lambda x: getName("jane@foo.com"))
d.addCallback(printResults)

reactor.callLater(1, finish)
reactor.run()
```

Note that the function called by `dbpool.runInteraction` uses the blocking cursor methods of the underlying database driver and runs in a separate thread. It must be a thread-safe function.

`dbpool.runInteraction` returns a `Deferred`. In this example, `_createUsersTable` implicitly returns `None`, which Twisted considers success, invoking the first callback in the callback chain.

More Practice and Next Steps

This chapter discussed how to interact with databases in a non-blocking fashion using Twisted's adbapi. adbapi provides an asynchronous interface to Python's DB-API 2.0 specification, which is defined in PEP 249 (*http://www.python.org/dev/peps/pep-0249/*). The methods in the asynchronous interface map directly to methods in the blocking API, so converting a service from blocking database queries to adbapi is straightforward.

For an example of how a large project uses Twisted's relational database support, check out the Buildbot continuous integration framework (*https://github.com/buildbot/build bot/*).

Twistar (*http://findingscience.com/twistar/*) is a library that builds an object-relational mapper (ORM) on top of adbapi.

CHAPTER 9

Authentication

Twisted comes with a protocol-independent, pluggable, asynchronous authentication system called *Cred* that can be used to add any type of authentication support to your Twisted server. Twisted also ships with a variety of common authentication mechanisms that you can use off the shelf through this system.

Because it is a general and extensible system, there are a number of components to understand and use in even a basic example. Getting over the initial learning curve will pay off for using Cred in real-world systems, so stick with me through the terminology and these examples.

Let me state up front that this is not a chapter on cryptography or password management best practices. This chapter uses hashing examples that are short and convenient for describing the capabilities of Twisted Cred with minimal overhead; if you want more information on securely managing user data, please consult a resource dedicated to this topic like *Secure Coding: Principles and Practices* (O'Reilly).

The Components of Twisted Cred

Before we get into the usage examples, there are a few terms that you should familiarize yourself with:

Credentials

Information used to identify and authenticate a user. Common credentials are a username and password, but they can be any data or object used to prove a user's identity, such as a certificate or challenge/response protocol. Objects that provide credentials implement `twisted.cred.credentials.ICredentials`.

Avatar

A business logic object in a server application that represents the actions and data available to a user. For example, an avatar for a mail server might be a mailbox object, an avatar for a web server might be a resource, and an avatar for an SSH server might be a remote shell.

Avatars implement an interface that inherits from `zope.interface.Interface`.

Avatar ID

A string returned by the credentials checker that identifies the avatar for a user. This is often a username, but it could be any unique identifier. Example avatar IDs are "Joe Smith", "joe@localhost", and "user926344".

Credentials checker

An object that takes credentials and attempts to verify them. The credentials checker is the bridge between the many ways credentials can be stored—for example, in a database, in a file, or in memory—and the rest of Cred.

If the credentials correctly identify a user, the credentials checker will return an avatar ID. Credentials checkers can also support anonymous access by returning `twisted.cred.checkers.ANONYMOUS`.

Credentials checkers implement the `twisted.cred.checker.ICredentialsCheck` `er` interface.

Realm

An object that provides access to all the possible avatars in an application. A realm will take an avatar ID identifying a specific user and return an avatar object that will work on behalf of that user. A realm can support multiple types of avatars, allowing different types of users to have access to different services on a server.

Realm objects implement the `twisted.cred.portal.IRealm` interface.

Portal

The portal mediates interactions between the many parts of Cred. At the protocol level, the only thing you need to use Cred is a reference to a portal. The portal's login method will authenticate users to the system.

The portal is not subclassed. Customization instead happens in the realm, credentials checkers, and avatars.

Twisted Cred: An Example

Now that we're primed with those definitions, let's look at a basic example. Example 9-1 shows an authenticating echo server.

Example 9-1. echo_cred.py

```
from zope.interface import implements, Interface

from twisted.cred import checkers, credentials, portal
from twisted.internet import protocol, reactor
```

```python
from twisted.protocols import basic

class IProtocolAvatar(Interface):
    def logout():
        """
        Clean up per-login resources allocated to this avatar.
        """

class EchoAvatar(object):
    implements(IProtocolAvatar)

    def logout(self):
        pass

class Echo(basic.LineReceiver):
    portal = None
    avatar = None
    logout = None

    def connectionLost(self, reason):
        if self.logout:
            self.logout()
            self.avatar = None
            self.logout = None

    def lineReceived(self, line):
        if not self.avatar:
            username, password = line.strip().split(" ")
            self.tryLogin(username, password)
        else:
            self.sendLine(line)

    def tryLogin(self, username, password):
        self.portal.login(credentials.UsernamePassword(username,
                                                       password),
                          None,
                          IProtocolAvatar).addCallbacks(self._cbLogin,
                                                        self._ebLogin)

    def _cbLogin(self, (interface, avatar, logout)):
        self.avatar = avatar
        self.logout = logout
        self.sendLine("Login successful, please proceed.")

    def _ebLogin(self, failure):
        self.sendLine("Login denied, goodbye.")
        self.transport.loseConnection()

    class EchoFactory(protocol.Factory):
        def __init__(self, portal):
            self.portal = portal
```

```
        def buildProtocol(self, addr):
            proto = Echo()
            proto.portal = self.portal
            return proto

class Realm(object):
    implements(portal.IRealm)

    def requestAvatar(self, avatarId, mind, *interfaces):
        if IProtocolAvatar in interfaces:
            avatar = EchoAvatar()
            return IProtocolAvatar, avatar, avatar.logout
        raise NotImplementedError(
            "This realm only supports the IProtocolAvatar interface.")

realm = Realm()
myPortal = portal.Portal(realm)
checker = checkers.InMemoryUsernamePasswordDatabaseDontUse()
checker.addUser("user", "pass")
myPortal.registerChecker(checker)

reactor.listenTCP(8000, EchoFactory(myPortal))
reactor.run()
```

To test the echo server, start it with *python echo_cred.py*. Connect to the server over *telnet* with *telnet localhost 8000*. To log in successfully, provide as the first line of client input *user pass*. You will then get a login message, and future lines will be echoed. Logging in with invalid credentials causes the server to send an invalid login message and terminate the connection. Here is an example client transcript:

```
$ telnet localhost 8000
Trying 127.0.0.1...
Connected to localhost.
Escape character is '^]'.
user pass
Login successful, please proceed.
Hi
Hi
Quit
Quit
^]
telnet> quit
Connection closed.
localhost:~ jesstess$ telnet localhost 8000
Trying 127.0.0.1...
Connected to localhost.
Escape character is '^]'.
foo bar
Login denied, goodbye.
Connection closed by foreign host.
```

Figure 9-1 illustrates Cred's authentication process diagrammatically.

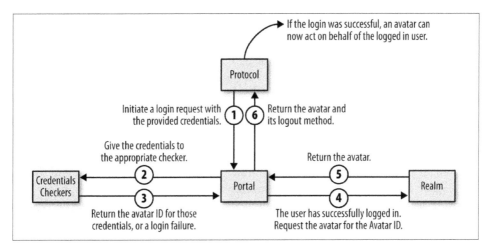

Figure 9-1. The Twisted Cred authentication process

The steps are:

1. Our protocol factory, `EchoFactory`, produces instances of `Echo` in its `buildProtocol` method, just like in Chapter 2. Unlike in Chapter 2, these protocols have a reference to a `Portal`.

   When we receive our first line from a connected client in `Echo.lineReceived`, we call our `Portal`'s `login` method to initiate a login request. `Portal.login`'s function signature is `login(credentials, mind, *interfaces)`. In detail, the three arguments it requires are:

   a. Credentials, in this case a `credentials.UsernamePassword` created from the username and password parsed out of the line received.

   b. A "mind" which is almost always `None`. We won't ever care about the mind in this book; if you are curious, the `Portal.login` documentation explains it.

   c. A list of avatar interfaces for which we are requesting authentication. This is usually a single interface (in this example, `IProtocolAvatar`).

2. The `Portal` hands off the credentials to the appropriate credentials checker based on the avatar interface requested.

   Each credentials checker exposes a set of `credentialInterfaces` for which it is able to authenticate. This example has only one checker, a toy `checkers.InMemoryUsernamePasswordDatabaseDontUse` that Twisted provides for learning about cred. This checker happens to support two types of credentials, `credentials.IUsernamePassword` and `credentials.IUsernameHashedPassword`. Because the call to `Portal.login` specified `credentials.UsernamePassword`, which implements credentials.IUsernamePassword, this credentials checker is able to authenticate the provided credentials.

3. A credentials checker returns a Deferred to the Portal, containing either an avatar ID if the credentials were correct or a login failure that terminates the login process and fires the errback chain for Portal.login. In this example, a failure would invoke Echo._ebLogin.

4. At this point, the user has successfully logged in. The Portal invokes the Realm's requestAvatar method, providing the avatar ID and the appropriate avatar interface.

5. requestAvatar returns a triple of avatar interface, avatar instance, and avatar logout method. If no per-login resources need to get cleaned up after a user logs out, the logout method can do nothing.

6. Portal.login returns a Deferred containing either the avatar interface, avatar instance, and avatar logout method triple or a login failure, as mentioned in Step 3. In this example, on success _cbLogin is called, sending a welcome message to the now-authenticated user.

Once authenticated, the echo client and server interact as in Chapter 2.

Credentials Checkers

With a minimal example under our belt, we can start to explore why cred's flexibility makes it so powerful. First, what if instead of using the toy in-memory checker we wanted to check the username and password against a file-based username and password database?

Twisted comes with a FilePasswordDB checker, so all we have to do is create a credentials file containing some usernames and passwords and swap in this FilePasswordDB checker:

```
-checker = checkers.InMemoryUsernamePasswordDatabaseDontUse()
-checker.addUser("user", "pass")
+checker = checkers.FilePasswordDB("passwords.txt")
```

FilePasswordDB's line format is customizable and defaults to username:password. Try running *echo_cred.py* with these changes and a test *passwords.txt*.

What if we wanted to use hashed passwords in our password file instead? FilePasswordDB takes an optional hash argument that it will apply to a password before comparing it to the hash stored on disk. To augment Example 9-1 to support hashed passwords, swap in:

```
+import hashlib
+def hash(username, password, passwordHash):
+    return hashlib.md5(password).hexdigest()
```

```
+
 realm = Realm()
 myPortal = portal.Portal(realm)
-checker = checkers.InMemoryUsernamePasswordDatabaseDontUse()
-checker.addUser("user", "pass")
+checker = checkers.FilePasswordDB("passwords.txt", hash=hash)
```

and use the same hash logic to generate the passwords in *passwords.txt*.

What if we wanted to store our passwords in a database?

Twisted does not ship with a database-backed credentials checker, so we'll need to write our own. It must implement the ICredentialsChecker interface, namely:

- Expose a class variable credentialInterfaces, which lists the credentials types the checker is able to check
- Implement the requestAvatarId method, which, given a set of credentials, must either authenticate the user and return its avatar ID or return a login failure

Example 9-2 implements a database-backed credentials checker.

Example 9-2. db_checker.py
```
from twisted.cred import error
from twisted.cred.checkers import ICredentialsChecker
from twisted.cred.credentials import IUsernameHashedPassword
from twisted.internet.defer import Deferred

from zope.interface import implements

class DBCredentialsChecker(object):
    implements(ICredentialsChecker)

    credentialInterfaces = (IUsernameHashedPassword,)

    def __init__(self, runQuery, query):
        self.runQuery = runQuery
        self.query = query

    def requestAvatarId(self, credentials):
        for interface in self.credentialInterfaces:
            if interface.providedBy(credentials):
                break
            else:
                raise error.UnhandledCredentials()

        dbDeferred = self.runQuery(self.query, (credentials.username,))
        deferred = Deferred()
        dbDeferred.addCallbacks(self._cbAuthenticate, self._ebAuthenticate,
                                callbackArgs=(credentials, deferred),
                                errbackArgs=(credentials, deferred))
        return deferred
```

```
    def _cbAuthenticate(self, result, credentials, deferred):
        if not result:
            deferred.errback(error.UnauthorizedLogin('User not in database'))
        else:
            username, password = result[0]
            if credentials.checkPassword(password):
                deferred.callback(credentials.username)
            else:
                deferred.errback(error.UnauthorizedLogin('Password mismatch'))

    def _ebAuthenticate(self, failure, credentials, deferred):
        deferred.errback(error.LoginFailed(failure))
```

To be database-agnostic, an instance of DBCredentialsChecker is initialized with an adbapi.ConnectionPool handle and the query to run to retrieve user credentials.

requestAvatarID returns a Deferred containing the avatar ID. The method takes a set of credentials, does a database lookup on the username from those credentials, and checks the password provided in the credentials against the one looked up in the database. On a password match, the Deferred's callback chain is invoked with credentials.username, which will be the avatar ID for this user. If the passwords don't match, the errback chain is invoked with cred.error.UnauthorizedLogin.

This checker expects credentials implementing IUsernameHashedPassword; the passwords are hashed before insertion into the database so the checker does not have access to the plain-text password, and credentials.checkPassword is invoked with the user-provided password to determine a match.

The only modifications needed to our original authenticating echo server are to swap in the DBCredentialsChecker and store hashed credentials in a database. Make these changes in *echo_server.py*:

First, at the top of the file define the hash used when inserting passwords into the database:

```
+import hashlib
+def hash(password):
+    return hashlib.md5(password).hexdigest()
```

Then, swap in the new type of credentials expected:

```
-        self.portal.login(credentials.UsernamePassword(
-                username, password),
+        self.portal.login(credentials.UsernameHashedPassword(
+                username, hash(password)),
```

Finally, swap in the new DBCredentialsChecker:

```
-checker = checkers.InMemoryUsernamePasswordDatabaseDontUse()
-checker.addUser("user", "pass")
+from twisted.enterprise import adbapi
```

```
+from db_checker import DBCredentialsChecker
+dbpool = adbapi.ConnectionPool("sqlite3", "users.db")
+checker = DBCredentialsChecker(
+    dbpool.runQuery,
+    query="SELECT username, password FROM users WHERE username = ?")
```

Where a simple `hash` implementation could be something similar to the function from our earlier modification to Example 9-1:

 Let me again remind you that this chapter is intentionally sticking to simple, concise examples. Don't use md5 to hash passwords. Don't store passwords in plaintext, do salt your passwords, and do use a cryptographically secure hash. If you want more information on how to securely manage user data, consult a resource dedicated to the topic. Your users will thank you!

Authentication in Twisted Applications

So far these Twisted Cred examples have used servers outside the Twisted application infrastructure discussed in Chapter 6. Twisted makes it easy to integrate authentication into applications deployed through *twistd* using the `AuthOptionMixin` class, and this is in fact where Twisted Cred really shines for providing a standard interface for swapping in and out authentication mechanisms decoupled from the business logic of your application.

As a concrete example, let's convert our authenticating echo server from Example 9-1 to a Twisted application. First, delete the realm, portal, and reactor code, which *twistd* and the plugin will handle instead, from that server file:

```
-realm = Realm()
-myPortal = portal.Portal(realm)
-checker = checkers.InMemoryUsernamePasswordDatabaseDontUse()
-checker.addUser("user", "pass")
-myPortal.registerChecker(checker)
-
-reactor.listenTCP(8000, EchoFactory(myPortal))
-reactor.run()
```

Then, create a plugin for this application using the same template from Example 6-4: in the directory containing the server application, create a *twisted* directory containing a *plugins* directory containing a file *echo_cred_plugin.py*. Example 9-3 has the code for this plugin.

Example 9-3. echo_cred_plugin.py

```
from twisted.application.service import IServiceMaker
from twisted.application import internet
from twisted.cred import credentials, portal, strcred
```

```
from twisted.plugin import IPlugin
from twisted.python import usage

from zope.interface import implements

from echo_cred import EchoFactory, Realm

class Options(usage.Options, strcred.AuthOptionMixin):
    supportedInterfaces = (credentials.IUsernamePassword,)
    optParameters = [["port", "p", 8000, "The port number to listen on."]]

class EchoServiceMaker(object):
    implements(IServiceMaker, IPlugin)
    tapname = "echo"
    description = "A TCP-based echo server."
    options = Options

    def makeService(self, options):
        """
        Construct a TCPServer from EchoFactory.
        """
        p = portal.Portal(Realm(), options["credCheckers"])
        return internet.TCPServer(int(options["port"]), EchoFactory(p))

serviceMaker = EchoServiceMaker()
```

This *echo_cred_plugin.py* looks exactly like the plugin from Example 6-4, with one difference: the authenticating EchoFactory needs to interface with a Portal, which in turn
needs to interface with a Realm and register credentials checkers. We want to be able to
configure the available credentials checkers from the command line, and to do this we
make our command-line Options class inherit from strcred.AuthOptionMixin.

Using AuthOptionMixin, all we have to do is enumerate the supported credentials types
in a supportedInterface class variable; and that gives us full access to command-line
credentials configuration. For this example, let's reuse a credentials type we've seen
before, credentials.IUsernamePassword.

With this AuthOptionMixin-enabled plugin in place, *twistd echo* grows command-line
authentication configuration and documentation:

```
$ twistd echo --help-auth
Usage: --auth AuthType[:ArgString]
For detailed help: --help-auth-type AuthType

AuthTypeArgString format
========================
memory  A colon-separated list (name:password:...)
file    Location of a FilePasswordDB-formatted file.
unix    No argstring required.
```

Let's try out our authenticating echo server with the *twistd* command-line version of checkers.InMemoryUsernamePasswordDatabaseDontUse from Example 9-1:

```
$ twistd -n echo --auth memory:user:pass:foo:bar
2012-12-01 14:04:11-0500 [-] Log opened.
2012-12-01 14:04:11-0500 [-] twistd 12.1.0 (/usr/bin/python 2.7.1) ...
2012-12-01 14:04:11-0500 [-] reactor class: twisted.internet.select...
2012-12-22 14:07:26-0500 [-] EchoFactory starting on 8000
2012-12-01 14:04:11-0500 [-] Starting factory <echo.EchoFactory ...
```

As before, we can now run *telnet localhost 8000* to play with this server.

With no application configuration, we can switch to authenticating against a password file like our *passwords.txt* by specifying the file auth type:

```
twistd -n echo --auth file:passwords.txt
```

On Unix, we can even use a built-in *unix* checker that "will attempt to use every resource available to authenticate against the list of users on the local UNIX system," which currently includes checking against */etc/passwd* and */etc/shadow*:

```
sudo twistd -n echo  --auth unix
```

You can then use your login username and password for this machine to authenticate to the echo server.

What if we wanted to add one of our custom checkers to this pool of available command-line checkers, alongside *memory*, *file*, and *unix*?

We do this with, as you might guess, a plugin. If you look in *twisted/plugins/* in the Twisted source code, you'll see a *cred_** file for each of the checkers we've used so far, as well as some others. Each Cred plugin implements and exposes a credentials checker factory. The list of credentials checkers available in *twistd --help-auth* is the set of checkers that implement the credentials interfaces specified in AuthOptionMixin's supportedInterfaces in your server's plugin file. In this echo example we specified credentials.IUsernamePassword, so the checkers available are those in *twisted/plugins/* that list IUsernamePassword in their credentialInterfaces.

So, to add our own checker for a particular credential interface to *twistd*, we would place the credentials checker and factory plugin in the *twisted/plugins/* subdirectory of our top-level project. After that, the checker will show up as an option in *twistd --help-auth*!

More Practice and Next Steps

This chapter discussed Twisted's Cred authentication system. In the Cred model, protocols authenticate users through a Portal, which mediates the validation of credentials against a credentials checker and returns an avatar which can act on behalf of the authenticated user. Cred uses the plugin system introduced in Chapter 6 to be a general and extensible framework.

Twisted's Web in 60 Seconds series (*https://twistedmatrix.com/documents/current/web/howto/web-in-60/*) walks through adding basic or digest HTTP authentication to a web server using Twisted Cred. For more practice, try adding authentication to one of your web servers from Chapter 4.

Conch, Twisted's SSH subproject, is discussed in Chapter 14 and makes extensive use of Twisted Cred.

CHAPTER 10

Threads and Subprocesses

A mantra from Chapter 3 bears repeating: Twisted does not automatically make your code asynchronous or nonblocking.

What does Twisted do? It provides nonblocking primitives for common networking, filesystem, and timer activities, which wrap underlying nonblocking APIs exposed by the operating system. Twisted programs are event-driven; they use callbacks and are structured differently from synchronous programs. Twisted provides the Deferred abstraction to help manage these callbacks.

Even though Twisted programs use this event-driven model, sometimes you'll still need to use threads or processes. This chapter covers some of the common cases and the relevant Twisted APIs.

Threads

In some cases—for example, when you're using a blocking third-party API—the functions you'd like to use in your Twisted program aren't under your control to be refactored into asynchronous ones using callbacks and Deferreds.

You are stuck with a blocking API, and you can't use it as-is or you'll block the entire event loop. To use it, you will need to make the blocking calls in threads. Twisted provides several methods related to making threaded calls, including:

callInThread
    Execute a blocking function in its own thread.

deferToThread
    Execute a blocking function in its own thread, and return the result as a Deferred.

In practice, deferToThread gets much more use than callInThread because you want a uniform interface to results, and Deferreds are that interface in Twisted programs.

Example 10-1 interleaves calls to a nonblocking function and a blocking function executed through deferToThread. It uses a convenient helper class for timing tasks: twisted.internet.task.LoopingCall. LoopingCall takes a function and its arguments and executes that function every interval provided to its start method. We used another method from the task module, deferLater, to execute a function after a specified time had elapsed in Example 4-10 .

Example 10-1. blocking.py

```
import time

from twisted.internet import reactor, threads
from twisted.internet.task import LoopingCall

def blockingApiCall(arg):
    time.sleep(1)
    return arg

def nonblockingCall(arg):
    print arg

def printResult(result):
    print result

def finish():
    reactor.stop()

d = threads.deferToThread(blockingApiCall, "Goose")
d.addCallback(printResult)

LoopingCall(nonblockingCall, "Duck").start(.25)

reactor.callLater(2, finish)
reactor.run()
```

Running this example produces:

```
$ python blocking.py
Duck
Duck
Duck
Duck
Duck
Goose
Duck
Duck
Duck
Duck
```

We can see by the interleaving of "Duck" and "Goose" output that by using threads.deferToThread we were able to make a blocking function call without blocking the reactor event loop.

Note that the reactor manages timer events, so LoopingCall only repeats function calls once the reactor is running.

We know that the reactor manages firing callbacks on Deferreds when events complete. What happens if we tweak the example to shut down the reactor before blockingApiCall has completed by changing the callLater line to reactor.callLater(.5, finish)?

```
$ python blocking.py
Duck
Duck
Duck
```

Because the reactor has shut down before the Deferred can be fired, Goose is never printed. To ensure that we wait until our deferToThread Deferred is done being processed before shutting down the reactor, we can make reactor.stop part of the callback chain, as shown in Example 10-2.

Example 10-2. blocking_revised.py

```
import time

from twisted.internet import reactor, threads
from twisted.internet.task import LoopingCall

def blockingApiCall(arg):
    time.sleep(1)
    return arg

def nonblockingCall(arg):
    print arg

def printResult(result):
    print result

def finish(result):
    reactor.stop()

d = threads.deferToThread(blockingApiCall, "Goose")
d.addCallback(printResult)
d.addCallback(finish)

LoopingCall(nonblockingCall, "Duck").start(.25)

reactor.run()
```

Twisted provides several other methods for running code in threads. They tend to come up less often, but it's good to know what your options are:

`callFromThread`
> From another thread, execute a function in the reactor thread.
>
> Use `callFromThread` to call reactor APIs from outside the reactor thread. For example, use `callFromThread` when:
>
> * writing data out through a transport from another thread
> * invoking a custom log observer from another thread
> * stopping the reactor from another thread

`callMultipleInThread`
> Execute a list of functions in the same thread.

`blockingCallFromThread`
> Execute the given function in the reactor thread, blocking the calling thread until the function has finished executing. If the function returns a `Deferred`, the result is translated into its synchronous equivalent: returning the result on success or raising an exception in the calling thread on failure.
>
> Use `blockingCallFromThread` if you need to interface with an API that expects synchronous results.

Subprocesses

Twisted provides a platform-independent API for running subprocesses in a non-blocking fashion through the reactor, with the output returned through a `Deferred`. This is one spot where Twisted shows its age: the Twisted API parallels the now-deprecated `commands` standard library module, which has been superseded by the `subprocess` module.

Running a Subprocess and Getting the Result

If all you need to do is run a process and get the output or return code, Twisted has convenience methods that make this easy: `getProcessOutput` and `getProcessValue`.

Example 10-3 shows a toy remote manpage server using `getProcessOutput`. It gets commands from a client, runs `man <command>` on each, and sends the output back to the client:

Example 10-3. manpage_server.py

```
import sys

from twisted.internet import protocol, utils, reactor
```

```
from twisted.protocols.basic import LineReceiver
from twisted.python import log

class RunCommand(LineReceiver):
    def lineReceived(self, line):
        log.msg("Man pages requested for: %s" % (line,))
        commands = line.strip().split(" ")
        output = utils.getProcessOutput("man", commands, errortoo=True)
        output.addCallback(self.writeSuccessResponse)

    def writeSuccessResponse(self, result):
        self.transport.write(result)
        self.transport.loseConnection()

class RunCommandFactory(protocol.Factory):
    def buildProtocol(self, addr):
        return RunCommand()

log.startLogging(sys.stdout)
reactor.listenTCP(8000, RunCommandFactory())
reactor.run()
```

As with our basic servers from Chapter 2, we create a `protocol.Factory` subclass `RunCommandFactory`, which creates instances of our custom `RunCommand` protocol as clients connect to the service. Since clients are sending line-delimited data, `RunCommand` subclasses `LineReceiver`. The server logs reactor activity and each client request to *stdout*.

When a line is received, `getProcessOutput` spawns a subprocess and returns a `Deferred` that will be fired when the process has completed. We attach a callback to `writeSuccessResponse`, which writes the command output to the underlying transport and then terminates the connection.

The environment in which a subprocess is executed can be customized through optional arguments to `getProcessOutput`. The full signature is `getProcessOutput(exe cutable, args=(), env={}, path=None, reactor=None, errortoo=False)`. Because we set `errortoo=True` above, *stderr* (for example, if a client requests a manpage for a non-existent command) is passed along with *stdout* to the success callback.

To execute a command and only retrieve the return code, use `getProcessValue`. It supports the same environment customization as `getProcessOutput` and has a nearly identical signature: `getProcessValue(executable, args=(), env={}, path=None, reactor=None)`.

Custom Process Protocols

If you need to do something beyond spawn a subprocess and get the output, you'll need to write an implementor of the `IProcessProtocol` (in practice, a subclass of `twist`

ed.internet.protocol.ProcessProtocol) that is invoked with reactor.spawnPro
cess. This includes writing data to the child process's stdin, executing subprocesses
that use redirection, and sending signals to the child process.

ProcessProtocol is structurally similar to the Protocol subclasses used when writing
basic clients and servers. It has a connectionMade method, as well as receive and connection lost methods for the child's file descriptors. The protocol callbacks are registered
with the reactor through spawnProcess, which has a similar but richer syntax than
getProcessOutput for specifying the child's environment.

Example 10-4 uses a custom EchoProcessProtocol to run the echo server application
from Example 6-3, killing the server after 10 seconds.

Example 10-4. twistd_spawnecho.py

```python
from twisted.internet import protocol, reactor

class EchoProcessProtocol(protocol.ProcessProtocol):
    def connectionMade(self):
        print "connectionMade called"
        reactor.callLater(10, self.terminateProcess)

    def terminateProcess(self):
        self.transport.signalProcess('TERM')

    def outReceived(self, data):
        print "outReceived called with %d bytes of data:\n%s" % (
            len(data), data)

    def errReceived(self, data):
        print "errReceived called with %d bytes of data:\n%s" % (
            len(data), data)

    def inConnectionLost(self):
        print "inConnectionLost called, stdin closed."

    def outConnectionLost(self):
        print "outConnectionLost called, stdout closed."

    def errConnectionLost(self):
        print "errConnectionLost called, stderr closed."

    def processExited(self, reason):
        print "processExited called with status %d" % (
            reason.value.exitCode,)

    def processEnded(self, reason):
        print "processEnded called with status %d" % (
            reason.value.exitCode,)
        print "All FDs are now closed, and the process has been reaped."
        reactor.stop()
```

```
pp = EchoProcessProtocol()

commandAndArgs = ["twistd", "-ny", "echo_server.tac"]
reactor.spawnProcess(pp, commandAndArgs[0], args=commandAndArgs)
reactor.run()
```

Run the example with *python twistd_spawnecho.py*. Then, in another terminal, connect to the spawned echo server with *telnet localhost 8000*. Entered text will be echoed back. After 10 seconds, the echo server terminates and the reactor is stopped, ending the parent process as well.

A transcript from the parent process might look like this:

```
$ python twisted_spawnprocess.py
connectionMade called
outReceived called with 295 bytes of data:
2012-12-01 14:04:11-0500 [-] Log opened.
2012-12-01 14:04:11-0500 [-] twistd 12.1.0 (/usr/bin/python 2.7.1) ...
2012-12-01 14:04:11-0500 [-] reactor class: twisted.internet.select...

outReceived called with 147 bytes of data:
2012-12-01 14:04:11-0500 [-] EchoFactory starting on 8000
2012-12-01 14:04:11-0500 [-] Starting factory <echo.EchoFactory ...

outReceived called with 62 bytes of data:
2012-12-01 14:04:20-0500 [-] Received SIGTERM, shutting down.

outReceived called with 52 bytes of data:
2012-12-01 14:04:20-0500 [-] (TCP Port 8000 Closed)

outReceived called with 89 bytes of data:
2012-12-01 14:04:20-0500 [-] Stopping factory <echo.EchoFactory ...

outReceived called with 51 bytes of data:
2012-12-01 14:04:20-0500 [-] Main loop terminated.

outReceived called with 47 bytes of data:
2012-12-01 14:04:20-0500 [-] Server Shut Down.

errConnectionLost called, stderr closed.
outConnectionLost called, stdout closed.
inConnectionLost called, stdin closed.
processExited called with status 0
processEnded called with status 0
All FDs are now closed, and the process has been reaped.
```

spawnProcess takes at minimum an instance of an implementor of the IProcessProtocol interface and the name of the executable to run, in this case *twistd*. This example also passes some command-line arguments to *twistd*: *-n* says to not daemonize, and *-y* is followed by the name of the TAC file to run.

The example uses a subclass of `ProcessProtocol` that, for illustration, overrides most of the class's methods:

`connectionMade`
> This method is called once the process has started and the `transport` has been set up for communicating with it. Data is written to the process's `stdin` with `self.transport.write`. You can also specify which file descriptor is written to with `self.transport.writeToChild`.

`outReceived`
> This method is called when data has arrived through the pipe for the process's *stdout*. Data is buffered and will arrive in chunks, so it may be appropriate to accumulate the data until `processEnded` has been called. `errReceived` similarly receives data written to the process's *stderr*.

`inConnectionLost, outConnectionLost, and errConnectionLost`
> These methods are called when the *stdin*, *stdout*, and *stderr* file descriptors are closed, respectively. The parent process might close *stdin* with `self.trans port.closeStdin` to indicate to the child that it shouldn't expect any more data from the parent, which would in turn invoke `inConnectionLost`. All three are called when the process terminates gracefully.

`processExited and processEnded`
> `processExited` is called when the process has exited. `processEnded` is the final callback invoked, when all file descriptors have closed. `processEnded` is thus an appropriate place to stop the reactor.

To illustrate sending signals to a subprocess, we use `self.transport.signalProcess` to send the server `SIGTERM` 10 seconds after the connection is made. Try sending `KILL` instead to see what happens if the process is not able to shut down gracefully.

More Practice and Next Steps

This chapter discussed how to use threads and subprocesses in a Twisted application in a nonblocking fashion.

Threads are most commonly required in a Twisted application when you are using a blocking third-party API. `deferToThread` executes a blocking function in its own thread and returns the result as a `Deferred`, giving you a consistent API even when working with other libraries.

Similarly, Twisted provides a platform-independent, `Deferred`-based API for running subprocesses as non-blocking events through the reactor, using `spawnProcess` and convenience functions like `getProcessOutput`. Custom process protocols subclass `protocol.ProcessProtocol` and are structurally quite similar to the `Protocol` implementations for network clients and servers.

The Twisted Core HOWTO discusses threads (*http://bit.ly/XSB0Ww*) and writing functions that return `Deferreds` (*http://bit.ly/XSB3l9*), which also gives additional examples of integrating blocking 3rd-party functions using `deferToThread`.

When we use Twisted's threading utilities, Twisted is managing allocations from a thread pool under the hood. For an example of using `twisted.python.threadpool` and the `twisted.internet.threads` APIs to wrap blocking third party functions, see the *twisted/enterprise/adbapi.py* asynchronous DB-API 2.0 implementation.

The Twisted Core HOWTO discusses processes (*http://bit.ly/XSB1d3*), and the *pty-serv* example in the Twisted Core examples directory (*http://bit.ly/XSB1dc*) shows a PTY server that spawns a shell upon connection.

ampoule (*http://bit.ly/XSB1de*) is a process pool implementation built on top of Twisted that provides an API mirroring the threading API.

CHAPTER 11

Testing

Because Twisted programs are event-driven and use `Deferreds` to wait for and handle events, we can't easily use standard testing frameworks like Python's `unittest` to write tests for them.

To handle this, Twisted comes with an extension of Python's `unittest` framework for testing event-driven Twisted programs, and a command-line utility for running them. These components comprise *Trial*, Twisted's testing framework.

Writing and Running Twisted Unit Tests with Trial

Tests that don't exercise event-driven logic import `twisted.trial.unittest` instead of `unittest` but otherwise look identical to traditional Python `unittest` tests.

Example 11-1 shows a single test case class called `MyFirstTestCase`, containing a single test called `test_something`, which makes an assertion using the Twisted version of `unittest`'s `TestCase.assertTrue`. Most `unittest` assertions have Twisted versions, and Trial has additional assertions for exercising `Failures`.

Example 11-1. test_foo.py

```
from twisted.trial import unittest

class MyFirstTestCase(unittest.TestCase):
    def test_something(self):
        self.assertTrue(True)
```

We can use the *trial* command-line utility that ships with Twisted to run the test file:

```
$ trial test_foo.py
test_foo
  MyFirstTestCase
    test_something ...                                          [OK]
```

```
---------------------------------------------------------------
Ran 1 tests in 0.002s

PASSED (successes=1)
```

We can run individual test classes by specifying the class name, as in:

```
trial test_foo.MyFirstTestCase
```

and run individual tests by specifying the path to the test, as in:

```
trial test_foo.MyFirstTestCase.test_something
```

Testing Protocols

Let's say we wanted to write a unit test suite for our echo protocol logic from Chapter 2 , reproduced Example 11-2 in for convenience.

Example 11-2. echo.py

```
from twisted.internet import protocol, reactor

class Echo(protocol.Protocol):
    def dataReceived(self, data):
        self.transport.write(data)

class EchoFactory(protocol.Factory):
    def buildProtocol(self, addr):
        return Echo()
```

These are unit tests; they shouldn't rely on making network connections. But how do we fake making a client connection?

Twisted provides helper modules in `twisted.test` for unit-testing clients and servers. Chief amongst them is `proto_helpers`, which has a `StringTransport` class for mocking transports. When a protocol uses an instance of `StringTransport`, instead of pushing bytes out through a network connection, they are written to a string which can easily be inspected.

Example 11-3 has a test case for the `Echo` protocol. It creates an instance of `EchoFactory`, uses that factory to build an instance of the `Echo` protocol, and sets the protocol's `transport` to an instance of `proto_helpers.StringTransport`. The protocol's `makeConnection` method is called to simulate a client connection, and `dataReceived` is called to simulate receiving client data. At that point, the transport should contain the echoed version of the fake client data, so we make an assertion on `transport.value()`.

Example 11-3. test_echo.py

```
from twisted.test import proto_helpers
from twisted.trial import unittest
```

```
from echo import EchoFactory

class EchoServerTestCase(unittest.TestCase):
    def test_echo(self):
        factory = EchoFactory()
        self.proto = factory.buildProtocol(("localhost", 0))
        self.transport = proto_helpers.StringTransport()

        self.proto.makeConnection(self.transport)
        self.proto.dataReceived("test\r\n")
        self.assertEqual(self.transport.value(), "test\r\n")
```

This idiom of:

1. Building a protocol instance

2. Giving it a mock transport

3. Faking client communication

4. Inspecting the mocked transport data

is very common when testing server functionality.

A handy feature built into trial is the generation of coverage information. If we pass --coverage to *trial*, it will generate coverage data for every Python module exercised during the test run and (by default) store it in *_trial_temp/*. Re-running the echo tests with *trial --coverage test_echo.py* and inspecting the resulting *_trial_temp/coverage/echo.cover*, we can see that we have full coverage of the echo module with this test:

```
$ cat _trial_temp/coverage/echo.cover
    1: from twisted.internet import protocol, reactor

    2: class Echo(protocol.Protocol):
    1:     def dataReceived(self, data):
    1:         self.transport.write(data)

    2: class EchoFactory(protocol.Factory):
    1:     def buildProtocol(self, addr):
    1:         return Echo()
```

As another example of mocking transports using proto_helpers.StringTransport, how about some unit tests for the chat protocol from Chapter 2 (reproduced in Example 11-4).

Example 11-4. chatserver.py

```
from twisted.internet.protocol import Factory
from twisted.protocols.basic import LineReceiver

class ChatProtocol(LineReceiver):
    def __init__(self, factory):
```

```
        self.factory = factory
        self.name = None
        self.state = "REGISTER"

    def connectionMade(self):
        self.sendLine("What's your name?")

    def connectionLost(self, reason):
        if self.name in self.factory.users:
            del self.factory.users[self.name]
            self.broadcastMessage("%s has left the channel." % (self.name,))

    def lineReceived(self, line):
        if self.state == "REGISTER":
            self.handle_REGISTER(line)
        else:
            self.handle_CHAT(line)

    def handle_REGISTER(self, name):
        if name in self.factory.users:
            self.sendLine("Name taken, please choose another.")
            return
        self.sendLine("Welcome, %s!" % (name,))
        self.broadcastMessage("%s has joined the channel." % (name,))
        self.name = name
        self.factory.users[name] = self
        self.state = "CHAT"

    def handle_CHAT(self, message):
        message = "<%s> %s" % (self.name, message)
        self.broadcastMessage(message)

    def broadcastMessage(self, message):
        for name, protocol in self.factory.users.iteritems():
            if protocol != self:
                protocol.sendLine(message)

class ChatFactory(Factory):
    def __init__(self):
        self.users = {}

    def buildProtocol(self, addr):
        return ChatProtocol(self)
```

As with the Echo protocol, we first set up an instance of the ChatFactory, build a protocol, and mock the transport. Since this is a more complicated protocol that will need
several tests, we can stick the setup work needed by every test in a setUp method, which
unittest will run before each test (there is a corresponding tearDown method to clean
up after each test).

After that, we can test each part of the state machine in its own unit test by calling lineReceived with the appropriate state-changing data and asserting on the contents of the mocked transport. Example 11-5 shows the start of a chat server test suite.

Example 11-5. Testing chatserver

```
from twisted.test import proto_helpers
from twisted.trial import unittest

from chatserver import ChatFactory

class ChatServerTestCase(unittest.TestCase):
    def setUp(self):
        self.factory = ChatFactory()
        self.proto = self.factory.buildProtocol(("localhost", 0))
        self.transport = proto_helpers.StringTransport()
        self.proto.makeConnection(self.transport)

    def test_connect(self):
        self.assertEqual(self.transport.value(),
                         "What's your name?\r\n")

    def test_register(self):
        self.assertEqual(self.proto.state, "REGISTER")
        self.proto.lineReceived("jesstess")
        self.assertIn("jesstess", self.proto.factory.users)
        self.assertEqual(self.proto.state, "CHAT")

    def test_chat(self):
        self.proto.lineReceived("jesstess")

        proto2 = self.factory.buildProtocol(("localhost", 0))
        transport2 = proto_helpers.StringTransport()
        proto2.makeConnection(transport2)

        self.transport.clear()
        proto2.lineReceived("adamf")

        self.assertEqual(self.transport.value(),
                         "adamf has joined the channel.\r\n")
```

To exercise the new user notification logic, we build a second fake client connection in test_chat.

trial --coverage test_foo.py shows a couple of untested code paths:

```
      1:      def connectionLost(self, reason):
>>>>>>            if self.name in self.factory.users:
>>>>>>                del self.factory.users[self.name]
>>>>>>                self.broadcastMessage("%s has left the channel." %
                                          (self.name,))
```

```
1:      def lineReceived(self, line):
3:          if self.state == "REGISTER":
3:              self.handle_REGISTER(line)
            else:
>>>>>>          self.handle_CHAT(line)

1:      def handle_REGISTER(self, name):
3:          if name in self.factory.users:
>>>>>>          self.sendLine("Name taken, please choose another.")
>>>>>>          return
3:          self.sendLine("Welcome, %s!" % (name,))
3:          self.broadcastMessage("%s has joined the channel." % (name,))
3:          self.name = name
3:          self.factory.users[name] = self
3:          self.state = "CHAT"

1:      def handle_CHAT(self, message):
>>>>>>      message = "<%s> %s" % (self.name, message)
>>>>>>      self.broadcastMessage(message)
```

To have complete test coverage, we'd need to exercise users leaving, nickname collision, and sending a chat message. What would those tests look like?

Tests and the Reactor

Eventually, you will find yourself needing to test something that involves the reactor: typically functions that return Deferreds or use methods like reactor.callLater that register time-based event handlers.

trial runs your test suite in a single thread, with a single reactor. This means that if a test ever leaves an event source (like a timer, socket, or misplaced Deferred) inside the reactor, it can affect future tests. At best, this causes them to fail. At worst, it causes tests to fail apparently randomly and sporadically, leaving you with a nightmare to debug.

This fact forces a basic rule when writing tests:

Leave the reactor as you found it.

This means:

- You cannot call reactor.run or reactor.stop inside a test.
- If a test invokes a function that returns a Deferred, that Deferred must be allowed to trigger. To ensure that this happens, return the Deferred. *trial* will keep the reactor running until the Deferred fires.

  A corollary is that a Deferred that is never triggered will cause your test suite to hang indefinitely.

- Events scheduled with reactor.callLater need to either happen or get cancelled before the test case finishes.

- Sockets—both client connections and listening server sockets—must be closed. Not having to worry about this is another reason why mocking connections is preferable in unit tests.

Operations to clean up the reactor often live in the `unittest.tearDown` test method.

Testing Deferreds

Example 11-6 is a concrete demonstration of what happens when a `Deferred` is left unfired in the reactor.

Example 11-6. test_deferred.py

```
from twisted.internet.defer import Deferred
from twisted.internet import reactor
from twisted.trial import unittest

class DeferredTestCase(unittest.TestCase):
    def slowFunction(self):
        d = Deferred()
        reactor.callLater(1, d.callback, ("foo"))
        return d

    def test_slowFunction(self):
        def cb(result):
            self.assertEqual(result, "foo")

        d = self.slowFunction()
        d.addCallback(cb)
```

`slowFunction` is a stand-in for any function that returns a `Deferred`. `test_slowFunction` is an attempt to test that when `slowFunction`'s callback chain is fired, it is with the result "foo".

Try running this test suite. You'll get something like:

```
$ trial test_deferred.DeferredTestCase
test_foo
  DeferredTestCase
    test_slowFunction ...                                           [ERROR]

===============================================================================
[ERROR]
Traceback (most recent call last):
Failure: twisted.trial.util.DirtyReactorAggregateError: Reactor was unclean.
DelayedCalls: (set twisted.internet.base.DelayedCall.debug = True to debug)
<DelayedCall 0x1010e1560 [0.9989798069s] called=0 cancelled=0 Deferred
  .callback(('foo',))>
```

`test_slowFunction` broke the rule: it invoked a function that returned a `Deferred` without returning the `Deferred`, causing the test to fail with a `DirtyReactorAggregateError`: Reactor was unclean.

To fix this test so it doesn't leave stray event sources in the reactor, return d.

`DBCredentialsChecker.requestAvatarId` from Example 9-2 is a method that returns a `Deferred`. Example 11-7 reproduces the full `DBCredentialsChecker` class for context. What would a test suite for `requestAvatarId` look like?

Example 11-7. db_checker.py

```python
class DBCredentialsChecker(object):
    implements(ICredentialsChecker)

    credentialInterfaces = (IUsernameHashedPassword,)

    def __init__(self, runQuery, query):
        self.runQuery = runQuery
        self.query = query

    def requestAvatarId(self, credentials):
        for interface in self.credentialInterfaces:
            if interface.providedBy(credentials):
                break
            else:
                raise error.UnhandledCredentials()

        dbDeferred = self.runQuery(self.query, (credentials.username,))
        deferred = Deferred()
        dbDeferred.addCallbacks(self._cbAuthenticate, self._ebAuthenticate,
                                callbackArgs=(credentials, deferred),
                                errbackArgs=(credentials, deferred))
        return deferred

    def _cbAuthenticate(self, result, credentials, deferred):
        if not result:
            deferred.errback(error.UnauthorizedLogin('User not in database'))
        else:
            username, password = result[0]
            if credentials.checkPassword(password):
                deferred.callback(credentials.username)
            else:
                deferred.errback(error.UnauthorizedLogin('Password mismatch'))

    def _ebAuthenticate(self, failure, credentials, deferred):
        deferred.errback(error.LoginFailed(failure))
```

Some good candidates for unit tests are:

- A test that a call to requestAvatarId with a matching username and password returns the username supplied in the credentials
- A test that a call to requestAvatarId with a known username but invalid password results in an UnauthorizedLogin error
- A test that a call to requestAvatarId with an unknown username results in an UnauthorizedLogin error

In lieu of setting up a test database as part of this test suite, we can mock the runQuery and query attributes to return fixed results.

Example 11-8 shows one possible implementation of the success test case. It instantiates a DBCredentialsChecker with a fakeRunqueryMatchingPassword that returns hard-coded correct credentials. A callback is attached to the Deferred returned by requestAvatarId to assert that the username in the supplied credentials is returned on a password match, and the Deferred is returned for Trial to ensure that it has time to fire.

Example 11-8. Testing DBCredentialsChecker

```
from twisted.trial import unittest
from twisted.cred import credentials
from twisted.cred.error import UnauthorizedLogin
from twisted.internet import reactor
from twisted.internet.defer import Deferred

from  db_checker import DBCredentialsChecker

class DBCredentialsCheckerTestCase(unittest.TestCase):

    def test_requestAvatarIdGoodCredentials(self):
        """
        Calling requestAvatarId with correct credentials returns the
        username.
        """
        def fakeRunqueryMatchingPassword(query, username):
            d = Deferred()
            reactor.callLater(0, d.callback, (("user", "pass"),))
            return d

        creds = credentials.UsernameHashedPassword("user", "pass")
        checker = DBCredentialsChecker(fakeRunqueryMatchingPassword,
                                        "fake query")
        d = checker.requestAvatarId(creds)

        def checkRequestAvatarCb(result):
            self.assertEqual(result, "user")
        d.addCallback(checkRequestAvatarCb)
        return d
```

Example 11-9 shows the two error test cases, which are structured quite similarly. They use a Twisted extension to Python's `unittest` assertions: `assertFailure`, which asserts that a `Deferred` fires with a `Failure` wrapping a particular type of `Exception`.

Example 11-9. Testing errors in DBCredentialsChecker

```python
def test_requestAvatarIdBadCredentials(self):
    """
    Calling requestAvatarId with invalid credentials raises an
    UnauthorizedLogin error.
    """
    def fakeRunqueryBadPassword(query, username):
        d = Deferred()
        reactor.callLater(0, d.callback, (("user", "badpass"),))
        return d

    creds = credentials.UsernameHashedPassword("user", "pass")
    checker = DBCredentialsChecker(fakeRunqueryBadPassword, "fake query")
    d = checker.requestAvatarId(creds)

    def checkError(result):
        self.assertEqual(result.message, "Password mismatch")
    return self.assertFailure(d, UnauthorizedLogin).addCallback(checkError)

def test_requestAvatarIdNoUser(self):
    """
    Calling requestAvatarId with credentials for an unknown user
    raises an UnauthorizedLogin error.
    """
    def fakeRunqueryMissingUser(query, username):
        d = Deferred()
        reactor.callLater(0, d.callback, ())
        return d

    creds = credentials.UsernameHashedPassword("user", "pass")
    checker = DBCredentialsChecker(fakeRunqueryMissingUser, "fake query")
    d = checker.requestAvatarId(creds)

    def checkError(result):
        self.assertEqual(result.message, "User not in database")
    return self.assertFailure(d, UnauthorizedLogin).addCallback(checkError)
```

Testing the Passage of Time

When you need to test code scheduled with `reactor.callLater`, for example protocol timeouts, you need to fake the passage of time. Twisted makes this easy with the `twisted.internet.task.Clock` class. `Clock` has its own `callLater` method, which replaces `reactor.callLater` in tests and can be advanced manually.

Because `Clock.callLater` replaces `reactor.callLater`, and we don't want to affect the global reactor while running tests, we need to parameterize the reactor (i.e., make the reactor an argument to a class's `__init__` method) so it can easily be replaced for testing.

Example 11-11 shows a test case for `EchoProcessProtocol` from Example 10-4. That class has been reproduced in Example 11-10 for convenience, with some changes, as discussed after the example code. `EchoProcessProtocol` terminates itself after 10 seconds using `reactor.callLater`, and we can use a `Clock` to exercise this behavior.

Example 11-10. pp.py

```
from twisted.internet import protocol, reactor

class EchoProcessProtocol(protocol.ProcessProtocol):
    def __init__(self, reactor):
        self.reactor = reactor

    def connectionMade(self):
        print "connectionMade called"
        self.reactor.callLater(10, self.terminateProcess)

    def terminateProcess(self):
        self.transport.signalProcess('TERM')

    def outReceived(self, data):
        print "outReceived called with %d bytes of data:\n%s" % (
            len(data), data)

    def errReceived(self, data):
        print "errReceived called with %d bytes of data:\n%s" % (
            len(data), data)

    def inConnectionLost(self):
        print "inConnectionLost called, stdin closed."

    def outConnectionLost(self):
        print "outConnectionLost called, stdout closed."

    def errConnectionLost(self):
        print "errConnectionLost called, stderr closed."

    def processExited(self, reason):
        print "processExited called with status %d" % (
            reason.value.exitCode,)

    def processEnded(self, reason):
        print "processEnded called with status %d" % (
            reason.value.exitCode,)
        print "All FDs are now closed, and the process has been reaped."
        self.reactor.stop()
```

Example 11-11. Testing EchoProcessProtocol

```
from twisted.test import proto_helpers
from twisted.trial import unittest
from twisted.internet import reactor, task

from pp import EchoProcessProtocol

class EchoProcessProtocolTestCase(unittest.TestCase):
    def test_terminate(self):
        """

        EchoProcessProtocol terminates itself after 10 seconds.
        """

        self.terminated = False

        def fakeTerminateProcess():
            self.terminated = True

        clock = task.Clock()
        pp = EchoProcessProtocol(clock)
        pp.terminateProcess = fakeTerminateProcess
        transport = proto_helpers.StringTransport()
        pp.makeConnection(transport)

        self.assertFalse(self.terminated)
        clock.advance(10)
        self.assertTrue(self.terminated)
```

Before writing this test case, we must parameterize the reactor used by `EchoProces` `sProtocol` by adding:

```
    def __init__(self, reactor):
        self.reactor = reactor
```

Then, in the test case, an instance of `EchoProcessProtocol` can be instantiated with an instance of `task.Clock`. A transport is set up, and assertions are made about the state of the protocol before and after a call to `clock.advance`, which simulates the passage of 10 seconds.

Parameterizing the reactor and using a `Clock` to simulate the passage of time is a common Twisted Trial idiom.

More Practice and Next Steps

This chapter introduced Twisted's Trial framework for unit-testing your Twisted applications.

The Twisted Core documentation includes a detailed introduction to test-driven development (*http://bit.ly/XSB1tA*) in Twisted and an overview of *trial* (*http://bit.ly/XSB3S9*). *trial* is, of course, itself written in Twisted, and test result processing can be customized using Twisted's plugin system. The *trial* code and tests live in *twisted/trial/*.

Twisted has a strict test-driven development policy: no code changes get merged without accompanying tests. Consequently, Twisted has an extensive test suite that is a great resource for examples of how to unit-test different scenarios. Tests live in the top-level *test/* directory as well as *test/* directories for each subproject.

For example, to see how Twisted Web's `Agent` interface is tested, including mocking the transport, testing timeouts, and testing errors, have a look at *twisted/web/test/ test_agent.py*. To see how to test a protocol like *twisted.words.protocols.irc*, check out *twisted/words/tests/test_irc.py*.

You can read about Twisted's test-driven development policy in detail on the Twisted website (*http://bit.ly/XSB1tM*).

Twisted publishes its own coverage information (*http://bit.ly/XSB48N*) as part of its continuous integration. Help improve Twisted by writing test cases!

PART III

More Protocols and More Practice

CHAPTER 12

Twisted Words

Twisted Words is an application-agnostic chat framework that gives you the building blocks to build clients and servers for popular chat protocols and to write new protocols.

Twisted comes with protocol implementations for IRC, Jabber (now XMPP, used by chat services like Google Talk and Facebook Chat), and AOL Instant Messenger's OSCAR.

To give you a taste of the Twisted Words APIs, this chapter will walk through implementations of an IRC client and server.

IRC Clients

An IRC client will look structurally quite similar to the basic clients from Chapter 2. The protocol will build upon `twisted.words.protocols.irc.IRCClient`, which inherits from `basic.LineReceiver` and implements the many user and channel operations supported by the protocol, including speaking and taking actions in private messages and in channels, managing your nickname, and setting channel properties.

Example 12-1 is an IRC echo bot that joins a particular channel on a particular network and echoes messages directed at the bot, as well as actions (like *me dances*) taken by other users in the channel.

Example 12-1. irc_echo_bot.py

```
from twisted.internet import reactor, protocol
from twisted.words.protocols import irc

import sys

class EchoBot(irc.IRCClient):
    nickname = "echobot"
```

```python
    def signedOn(self):
        # Called once the bot has connected to the IRC server
        self.join(self.factory.channel)

    def privmsg(self, user, channel, msg):
        # Despite the name, called when the bot receives any message,
        # be it a private message or in a channel.
        user = user.split('!', 1)[0]
        if channel == self.nickname:
            # This is a private message to me; echo it.
            self.msg(user, msg)
        elif msg.startswith(self.nickname + ":"):
            # This message started with my nickname and is thus
            # directed at me; echo it.
            self.msg(channel, user + ":" + msg[len(self.nickname + ":"):])

    def action(self, user, channel, action):
        # Called when a user in the channel takes an action (e.g., "/me
        # dances"). Imitate the user.
        self.describe(channel, action)

class EchoBotFactory(protocol.ClientFactory):
    def __init__(self, channel):
        self.channel = channel

    def buildProtocol(self, addr):
        proto = EchoBot()
        proto.factory = self
        return proto

    def clientConnectionLost(self, connector, reason):
        # Try to reconnect if disconnected.
        connector.connect()

    def clientConnectionFailed(self, connector, reason):
        reactor.stop()

network = sys.argv[1]
port = int(sys.argv[2])
channel = sys.argv[3]
reactor.connectTCP(network, port, EchoBotFactory(channel))
reactor.run()
```

Almost all of the work is done by the underlying irc.IRCClient implementation; the only substantial customizations are to the privmsg and action methods, to give the bot its echo behavior.

This bot will automatically try to reconnect to the service if disconnected. This behavior is achieved by re-establishing the connection with connector.connect in the EchoBotFactory's clientConnectionLost method.

The bot takes as command-line arguments the IRC server, port, and channel it should join. For example, to bring this bot into the *#twisted-bots* channel on the Freenode IRC network, run:

```
python irc_echo_bot.py irc.freenode.net 6667 twisted-bots
```

Join that channel as well to see your bot in action. Here's an example transcript:

```
21:11 -!- echobot [~echobot@] has joined #twisted-bots
21:11 <jesstess> echobot: Hi!
21:11 < echobot> jesstess: Hi!
21:12 <jesstess> adamf: I just finished reading RFC 959 and could use a drink.
21:20  * jesstess goes to sleep
21:20  * echobot goes to sleep
21:25 -!- echobot_ [~echobot@] has quit [Remote host closed the connection]
```

IRC Servers

The Twisted Words server APIs have had a lot less development and use than the client APIs. Support exists for bare-bones services, but the rest is up to the developer. If you are interested in contributing to Twisted, this is an area that could use your love!

Twisted Words servers build upon `twisted.words.service`, which exposes chat-specific authentication using the Twisted Cred model from Chapter 9 as well as an `IRCFactory` that generates instances of the `IRCUser` protocol.

Example 12-2 shows an IRC server that listens for IRC connections on port 6667 and authenticates users based on the contents of a colon-delimited *passwords.txt* file.

Example 12-2. irc_server.py

```
from twisted.cred import checkers, portal
from twisted.internet import reactor
from twisted.words import service

wordsRealm = service.InMemoryWordsRealm("example.com")
wordsRealm.createGroupOnRequest = True

checker = checkers.FilePasswordDB("passwords.txt")
portal = portal.Portal(wordsRealm, [checker])

reactor.listenTCP(6667, service.IRCFactory(wordsRealm, portal))
reactor.run()
```

`InMemoryWordsRealm` implements the `IChatService` interface, which describes adding users and groups (in our case, channels) to the service. As a `Realm` in the Twisted Cred sense, it produces instances of avatars—in this case, `IRCUsers`.

Setting `createGroupOnRequest` = `True` allows users to create new IRC channels on the fly.

To test this server, first create a *passwords.txt* file containing a few colon-delimited credentials. Then run:

```
python irc_server.py
```

and connect to the service locally with your favorite IRC client. Here, we'll use the terminal-based *irssi* client and connect with the username *jesstess* and password *pass*, as specified in *passwords.txt*:

```
irssi -c localhost -p 6667 -n jesstess -w pass
```

Our echo bot can get in on the action, too! We can either configure our credentials checker to allow anonymous login, or give the bot a password. The latter is simplest for this demonstration—we can just add a `password` class variable alongside the `nickname` class variable and add those credentials to *passwords.txt*. Then we run the echo bot with *python irc_echo_bot.py localhost 6667 twisted-bots* to join the local *#twisted-bots* channel upon login.

Figures 12-1, 12-2, and 12-3 show some screenshots of the *irssi* IRC client and the echo bot interacting on the Twisted IRC server. Various basic commands, like `/LIST` and `/WHOIS`, work off the shelf, but we can also customize them by subclassing `twisted.words.service.IRCUser` and implementing the `irc_*` handler for the command. We'd then subclass `twisted.words.service.IRCFactory` to serve instances of our `IRCUser` protocol subclass.

```
Irssi v0.8.15   http://www.irssi.org
20:19 -!- Irssi: Looking up localhost
20:19 -!- Irssi: Connecting to localhost [127.0.0.1] port 6667
20:19 -!- Irssi: Connection to localhost established
20:19 -!- - example.com Message of the Day -
20:19 -!- End of /MOTD command.
20:19 -!- connected to Twisted IRC
20:19 -!- Your host is example.com, running version 12.0.0
20:19 -!- This server was created on Tue Feb 26 20:19:16 2013
20:19 -!- example.com 12.0.0 w n
[20:20] [jesstess] [1:localhost (change with ^X)]
[(status)] /join #twisted-bots
```

Figure 12-1. Connecting to the Twisted IRC server using irssi

```
20:20 -!- ████████ [jesstess@example.com] has joined #twisted-bots
20:20 [Users #twisted-bots]
20:20 [ jesstess]
20:20 -!- Irssi: #twisted-bots: Total of 1 nicks [0 ops, 0 halfops, 0 voices, 1 normal]
20:21 -!- ████████ [echobot@example.com] has joined #twisted-bots
20:21 < jesstess> echobot: nice to see you!
20:21 < ███████> jesstess: nice to see you!
[20:22] [jesstess] [2:localhost/#twisted-bots] [Act: 1]
[#twisted-bots]
```

Figure 12-2. Talking with the echo bot in #twisted-bots

```
Irssi v0.8.15   http://www.irssi.org
20:23 -!- Your host is example.com, running version 12.0.0
20:23 -!- This server was created on Tue Feb 26 20:19:16 2013
20:23 -!- example.com 12.0.0 w n
20:23 -!- twisted-bots 1
20:23 -!- End of /LIST
20:23 -!- echobot [echobot@example.com]
20:23 -!-  ircname  : echobot
20:23 -!-  server   : example.com [Hi mom!]
20:23 -!-  idle     : 0 days 0 hours 1 mins 39 secs [signon: Tue Feb 26 20:21:29 2013]
20:23 -!-  channels : #twisted-bots
20:23 -!- End of WHOIS
[20:23] [jesstess] [1:localhost (change with ^X)]
[(status)]
```

Figure 12-3. Issuing some basic commands against the Twisted IRC server

Some examples of IRC commands implemented by IRCUser and its superclass twisted.words.protocols.irc.IRC are:

irc_JOIN
 Join a set of channels.

irc_LIST
 List the channels on a server.

irc_MODE
 Set user and channel modes.

irc_NAMES
 Request who is in a set of channels.

irc_NICK
 Set your nickname.

irc_OPER
 Authenticate as an IRC operator.

`irc_PART`
: Leave a set of channels.

`irc_PASS`
: Set a password.

`irc_PING`
: Send a ping message.

`irc_PRIVMSG`
: Send a private message.

`irc_QUIT`
: Disconnect from the server.

`irc_TOPIC`
: Set the topic for a channel.

`irc_USER`
: Set your real name.

`irc_WHO`
: Request a list of users matching a particular name.

`irc_WHOIS`
: Request information about a set of nicknames.

More Practice and Next Steps

This chapter introduced the Twisted Words subproject through an example IRC client and server. Twisted Words was built to be a general and extensible multiprotocol chat framework. Primitive support exists for popular protocols like IRC, XMPP, and AOL Instant Messenger's OSCAR, and it is also easy to add new protocols. The Twisted Words documentation (*http://bit.ly/XSB4FI*) has a short development guide and several examples, including XMPP and AOL Instant Messenger clients and a demo *curses*-based IRC client.

Wokkel (*http://bit.ly/XSB74n*), a third-party library built on top of Twisted Words, provides substantial enhancements to Twisted's Jabber/XMPP protocol support. Twisted also has a mailing list dedicated to Twisted Jabber development (*http://bit.ly/XSB4FW*).

Twisted Words is one of the less-developed Twisted subprojects, and there is consequently a lot of low-hanging fruit in this area for folks interested in contributing to Twisted. In particular, an expanded developer guide and more server examples would be welcome additions. See tickets with the "words" component in the Twisted bug tracker for open Twisted Words issues.

CHAPTER 13

Twisted Mail

Twisted comes with support for building clients and servers for the three big email protocols in common use today: SMTP, IMAP, and POP3.

Each of these protocols has a lot of components and is meticulously documented in multiple RFCs; covering the ins and outs of mail servers and clients could be a book in and of itself. The goal for this chapter is instead to give you broad-strokes familiarity with the protocols and the APIs Twisted provides for them, through some simple but runnable and tinker-friendly examples. By the end, you should have a good idea of what you'd need to do to build arbitrary email applications in Twisted.

To describe in brief the main uses for each of these protocols:

SMTP

> SMTP, the Simple Mail Transfer Protocol, is for sending mail; when you send an e-mail from the Gmail web interface, your Thunderbird desktop app, or the mail app on your smartphone, that message is probably getting sent over SMTP.

IMAP

> IMAP, the Internet Message Access Protocol, is used for remote access, storage, and management of email messages. Remote management makes it easy to read and send mail from more than one place. The fact that you see the same messages on your phone, web interface, and desktop app is probably because your email provider is using IMAP for remote management.

POP3

> POP3, the Post Office Protocol version 3, is an older and simpler protocol than IMAP, but still prevalent. POP3 does one thing, and does it well: it allows a user to log into a mail server and download her messages, optionally deleting the copies on the server afterwards. If you've ever exported your Gmail mail, it was probably using POP3.

SMTP Clients and Servers

The standard protocol for sending mail on the Internet is the Simple Mail Transfer Protocol (SMTP). SMTP allows one computer to transfer email messages to another computer using a standard set of commands. Mail clients use SMTP to send outgoing messages, and mail servers use SMTP to forward messages to their final destination. The current specification for SMTP is defined in RFC 2821 (*http://bit.ly/XSB7l3*).

The SMTP Protocol

SMTP is a plain-text protocol. To get a feel for what the underlying Twisted protocol implementation is doing, we can talk the protocol to an SMTP server to forge emails!

To do this, we need to know the IP address or hostname of an SMTP server. You may know one from configuring your email setup at work or school. If not, as it happens, Google runs open SMTP servers, so we can look up and use one of them.

The *nslookup* command makes it easy to query domain name servers for a host or domain. In this case, we'd like to look up some mail exchange (MX) servers for *google.com*:

```
$ nslookup
> set type=MX
> google.com
Server:192.168.1.1
Address:192.168.1.1#53

Non-authoritative answer:
google.commail exchanger = 10 aspmx.l.google.com.
google.commail exchanger = 50 alt4.aspmx.l.google.com.
google.commail exchanger = 20 alt1.aspmx.l.google.com.
google.commail exchanger = 30 alt2.aspmx.l.google.com.
google.commail exchanger = 40 alt3.aspmx.l.google.com.
```

This query tells us that at the time of this writing, *aspmx.l.google.com* and friends are available mail servers. We can use *telnet* to connect to this server on port 25, the traditional SMTP port, and speak SMTP to forge an email from a secret admirer to a Gmail user:

```
$ telnet aspmx.l.google.com 25
Trying 74.125.131.27...
Connected to aspmx.l.google.com.
Escape character is '^]'.
220 mx.google.com ESMTP a4si49083129vdi.29
helo secretadmirer@example.com
250 mx.google.com at your service
mail from: <secretadmirer@example.com>
250 2.1.0 OK a4si49083129vdi.29
rcpt to: <twistedechobot@gmail.com>
250 2.1.5 OK a4si49083129vdi.29
```

```
data
354  Go ahead a4si49083129vdi.29
From: "Secret Admirer" <secretadmirer@example.com>
Subject: Roses are red

Violets are blue
Twisted is helping
Forge emails to you!
.
250 2.0.0 OK 1357178694 a4si49083129vdi.29
```

The preceding interaction sends an email that appears to be from *secretadmirer@example.com* to *twistedechobot@gmail.com*. Go ahead and try it yourself—note that the email will almost certainly end up in the recipients' spam box because it wasn't sent with the authentication headers Gmail is expecting.

The fourth line of that transcript, `220 mx.google.com ESMTP a4si49083129vdi.29`, shows that the SMTP server was talking to us over Extended SMTP (ESMTP), which most modern clients and servers use and which we'll focus on in this chapter.

Sending Emails Using SMTP

The Twisted Mail equivalent of `getPage` from Chapter 3—the quick way to send an email—is `twisted.mail.smtp.sendmail`.

Example 13-1 shows the `sendmail` equivalent of sending the preceding email.

Example 13-1. Sending an email over SMTP with sendmail

```
import sys

from email.mime.text import MIMEText

from twisted.internet import reactor
from twisted.mail.smtp import sendmail
from twisted.python import log

log.startLogging(sys.stdout)

host = "aspmx.l.google.com"
sender = "secretadmirer@example.com"
recipients = ["twistedechobot@gmail.com"]

msg = MIMEText("""Violets are blue
Twisted is helping
Forge e-mails to you!
""")
msg["Subject"] = "Roses are red"
msg["From"] = '"Secret Admirer" <%s>' % (sender,)
msg["To"] = ", ".join(recipients)
```

```
deferred = sendmail(host, sender, recipients, msg.as_string(), port=25)
deferred.addBoth(lambda result: reactor.stop())

reactor.run()
```

The email is constructed using the Python standard library's email module. sendmail spins up an instance of twisted.mail.smtp.SMTPSenderFactory under the hood, which sends the message to the specified SMTP host on port 25.

SMTP Servers

Example 13-2 is a simple SMTP server that listens for SMTP clients on port 2500 and prints received messages to *stdout*. It will accept mail from any sender but will only process mail to recipients on *localhost*.

Example 13-2. localhost SMTP server, smtp_server.py

```
import sys

from email.Header import Header
from zope.interface import implements

from twisted.internet import defer, reactor
from twisted.mail import smtp
from twisted.python import log

class StdoutMessageDelivery(object):
    implements(smtp.IMessageDelivery)

    def __init__(self, protocol):
        self.protocol = protocol

    def receivedHeader(self, helo, origin, recipients):
        clientHostname, _ = helo
        myHostname = self.protocol.transport.getHost().host
        headerValue = "from %s by %s with ESMTP ; %s" % (
            clientHostname, myHostname, smtp.rfc822date())
        return "Received: %s" % Header(headerValue)

    def validateFrom(self, helo, origin):
        # Accept any sender.
        return origin

    def validateTo(self, user):
        # Accept recipients @localhost.
        if user.dest.domain == "localhost":
            return StdoutMessage
        else:
            log.msg("Received email for invalid recipient %s" % user)
            raise smtp.SMTPBadRcpt(user)
```

```
class StdoutMessage(object):
    implements(smtp.IMessage)

    def __init__(self):
        self.lines = []

    def lineReceived(self, line):
        self.lines.append(line)

    def eomReceived(self):
        print "New message received:"
        print "\n".join(self.lines)
        self.lines = None
        return defer.succeed(None)

class StdoutSMTPFactory(smtp.SMTPFactory):

    def buildProtocol(self, addr):
        proto = smtp.ESMTP()
        proto.delivery = StdoutMessageDelivery(proto)
        return proto

log.startLogging(sys.stdout)

reactor.listenTCP(2500, StdoutSMTPFactory())
reactor.run()
```

Run this example with *python smtp_server.py*. We can then tweak our sendmail client from Example 13-1 to interact with this *localhost* server. Just change the host to *localhost*, the recipient to a *localhost* user, and the port to 2500:

```
-host = "localhost"
+host = "aspmx.l.google.com"
 sender = "secretadmirer@example.com"
-recipients = ["recipient@localhost"]
+recipients = ["twistedechobot@gmail.com"]

-deferred = sendmail(host, sender, recipients, msg.as_string(), port=25)
+deferred = sendmail(host, sender, recipients, msg.as_string(), port=2500)
```

Then run the SMTP client and watch the server log the message to *stdout*:

```
2013-01-05 21:17:54-0500 [ESMTP,0,127.0.0.1] Receiving message for delivery:
  from=secretadmirer@example.com to=['recipient@localhost']
2013-01-05 21:17:54-0500 [ESMTP,0,127.0.0.1] New message received:
2013-01-05 21:17:54-0500 [ESMTP,0,127.0.0.1] Received: from localhost by
  127.0.0.1 with ESMTP ; Sat, 05 Jan 2013 21:17:54 -0500
2013-01-05 21:17:54-0500 [ESMTP,0,127.0.0.1] Content-Type: text/plain;
  charset="us-ascii"
2013-01-05 21:17:54-0500 [ESMTP,0,127.0.0.1] MIME-Version: 1.0
2013-01-05 21:17:54-0500 [ESMTP,0,127.0.0.1] Content-Transfer-Encoding: 7bit
2013-01-05 21:17:54-0500 [ESMTP,0,127.0.0.1] Subject: Roses are red
2013-01-05 21:17:54-0500 [ESMTP,0,127.0.0.1] From: "Secret Admirer"
```

```
          <secretadmirer@example.com>
2013-01-05 21:17:54-0500 [ESMTP,0,127.0.0.1] To: recipient@localhost
2013-01-05 21:17:54-0500 [ESMTP,0,127.0.0.1]
2013-01-05 21:17:54-0500 [ESMTP,0,127.0.0.1] Violets are blue
2013-01-05 21:17:54-0500 [ESMTP,0,127.0.0.1] Twisted is helping
2013-01-05 21:17:54-0500 [ESMTP,0,127.0.0.1] Forge emails to you!
```

The SMTP server has three main components:

1. An SMTP protocol factory

2. An implementor of `smtp.IMessageDelivery`, which describes how to process a message

3. An implementor of `smtp.IMessage`, which describes what to do with a received message

Like all of the other protocol factories we've seen, `StdoutSMTPFactory` inherits from a base factory and implements `buildProtocol`, which returns an instance of the `smtp.ESMTP` protocol. The one detail you must set for SMTP is is the protocol's `delivery` instance variable.

Our delivery class is `StdoutMessageDelivery`. Implementors of the `IMessageDelivery` interface must implement three methods: `validateFrom`, `validateTo`, and `receivedHeader`. `validateFrom` and `validateTo` restrict the sender and recipient allowed by the server. In our case we only accept messages destined for a user at *localhost*.

`receivedHeader` returns a `Received` header string: metadata required by the SMTP RFC to be added to the message headers for each SMTP server that processes a message. This allows us to trace the route a message took to get from its sender to us. We rely on `email.Header` from the Python standard library to format the header for us.

Storing Mail

We've got an SMTP server that can validate and accept mail, but it would be more useful if we could store that mail so we could access it in the future. To do this, we can revamp our SMTP server to write messages to disk in a popular mail storage format called *Maildir*.

Maildir structures each mail folder (e.g., Inbox, Trash) as a directory, and each message is its own file. Twisted comes with Maildir support.

We'll still need the same three SMTP server components: an SMTP protocol factory and an implementor of `smtp.IMessageDelivery`, which will be almost unchanged, and an implementor of `smtp.IMessage`, which will be quite different since what we do with a received message is exactly what we're changing. Example 13-3 shows this revised server.

Example 13-3. SMTP Maildir server

```
import os
import sys

from email.Header import Header
from zope.interface import implements

from twisted.internet import reactor
from twisted.mail import smtp, maildir
from twisted.python import log

class LocalMessageDelivery(object):
    implements(smtp.IMessageDelivery)

    def __init__(self, protocol, baseDir):
        self.protocol = protocol
        self.baseDir = baseDir

    def receivedHeader(self, helo, origin, recipients):
        clientHostname, clientIP = helo
        myHostname = self.protocol.transport.getHost().host
        headerValue = "from %s by %s with ESMTP ; %s" % (
            clientHostname, myHostname, smtp.rfc822date())
        return "Received: %s" % Header(headerValue)

    def validateFrom(self, helo, origin):
        # Accept any sender.
        return origin

    def _getAddressDir(self, address):
        return os.path.join(self.baseDir, "%s" % address)

    def validateTo(self, user):
        # Accept recipients @localhost.
        if user.dest.domain == "localhost":
            return lambda: MaildirMessage(
                self._getAddressDir(str(user.dest)))
        else:
            log.msg("Received email for invalid recipient %s" % user)
            raise smtp.SMTPBadRcpt(user)

class MaildirMessage(object):
    implements(smtp.IMessage)

    def __init__(self, userDir):
        if not os.path.exists(userDir):
            os.mkdir(userDir)
        inboxDir = os.path.join(userDir, 'Inbox')
        self.mailbox = maildir.MaildirMailbox(inboxDir)
        self.lines = []

    def lineReceived(self, line):
```

```
            self.lines.append(line)

    def eomReceived(self):
        print "New message received."
        self.lines.append('') # Add a trailing newline.
        messageData = '\n'.join(self.lines)
        return self.mailbox.appendMessage(messageData)

    def connectionLost(self):
        print "Connection lost unexpectedly!"
        # Unexpected loss of connection; don't save.
        del(self.lines)

class LocalSMTPFactory(smtp.SMTPFactory):
    def __init__(self, baseDir):
        self.baseDir = baseDir

    def buildProtocol(self, addr):
        proto = smtp.ESMTP()
        proto.delivery = LocalMessageDelivery(proto, self.baseDir)
        return proto

log.startLogging(sys.stdout)

reactor.listenTCP(2500, LocalSMTPFactory("/tmp/mail"))
reactor.run()
```

To test this Maildir-capable server, create a */tmp/mail* or equivalent test directory, run the server, and re-run the sendmail client example. You should see log output like:

```
2013-01-05 21:39:23-0500 [ESMTP,0,127.0.0.1] New message received.
```

and the creation of a */tmp/mail/recipient@localhost/Inbox/* directory containing *cur*, *new*, and *tmp* directories.

Inside *new* you'll find a file like *1357439963.M1476850P45295Q2.localhost* containing your message.

This SMTP client and server pair are a good starting point for experimenting with the Twisted Mail APIs and building up more full-fledged SMTP applications.

IMAP Clients and Servers

The Internet Message Access Protocol (IMAP) was designed to allow for remote access, storage, and management of email messages. This ability to store messages on a central server is useful for a couple of reasons. First, it makes email available in more than one place. If your mail is on an IMAP server, you can switch between your desktop and your laptop and still access your mail. Second, it makes it easier to administer email for workgroups and corporations. Instead of having to track and back up email across hundreds of hard drives, it can be managed in a single, central place.

The specification for the current version of IMAP (version 4, revision 1) is defined in RFC 3501 (*http://bit.ly/XSB5cQ*). IMAP is a powerful but complicated protocol, and the RFC takes up more than 100 pages. It's the kind of protocol that would be a ton of work to implement yourself. Fortunately, the Twisted developers have written a complete IMAP implementation, which provides a nice API for working with IMAP servers.

For a taste of working with IMAP, let's write an IMAP server that can serve the Maildir messages gathered by the SMTP client we created earlier, and an IMAP client to retrieve them.

IMAP Servers

The goal of this book is to help you develop a fluency with Twisted's primitives and not to torture you with the details of any specific protocol, so given IMAP's complexity, we'll stick with developing the absolute minimal viable IMAP server. It will know how to serve messages by sequence number and do basic Twisted Cred authentication.

First, take a few moments to think about what components our authenticating IMAP server will have based on what you know about writing Twisted servers in general, about writing mail servers particularly, and about authentication. You already know much of this!

First, we need a protocol—in this case, a subclass of `imap4.IMAP4Server`—and a protocol factory subclassing `protocol.Factory`. To authenticate, we'll also need a `Realm`, a `Portal`, and a credentials checker.

To implement a minimal IMAP server we'll need three more components:

1. An implementor of `imap4.IMessage`, which represents a message.

2. An implementor of `imap4.IMailbox`, which represents an individual mailbox. Users can check, add messages to, and expunge messages from their mailboxes. The mailbox must understand how a message is stored—in our case, in the Maildir format.

3. An implementor of `imap4.IAccount`, which is the avatar—the business logic object in the Twisted Cred model. Through this mail account, users can manage and list their mailboxes.

Example 13-4 shows a minimal IMAP server implementation.

Example 13-4. IMAP Maildir server, imapserver.py

```
import email
import os
import random
from StringIO import StringIO
import sys
from zope.interface import implements
```

```
from twisted.cred import checkers, portal
from twisted.internet import protocol, reactor
from twisted.mail import imap4, maildir
from twisted.python import log

class IMAPUserAccount(object):
    implements(imap4.IAccount)

    def __init__(self, userDir):
        self.dir = userDir

    def _getMailbox(self, path):
        fullPath = os.path.join(self.dir, path)
        if not os.path.exists(fullPath):
            raise KeyError, "No such mailbox"
        return IMAPMailbox(fullPath)

    def listMailboxes(self, ref, wildcard):
        for box in os.listdir(self.dir):
            yield box, self._getMailbox(box)

    def select(self, path, rw=False):
        return self._getMailbox(path)

class ExtendedMaildir(maildir.MaildirMailbox):
    def __iter__(self):
        return iter(self.list)

    def __len__(self):
        return len(self.list)

    def __getitem__(self, i):
        return self.list[i]

class IMAPMailbox(object):
    implements(imap4.IMailbox)

    def __init__(self, path):
        self.maildir = ExtendedMaildir(path)
        self.listeners = []
        self.uniqueValidityIdentifier = random.randint(1000000, 9999999)

    def getHierarchicalDelimiter(self):
        return "."

    def getFlags(self):
        return []

    def getMessageCount(self):
        return len(self.maildir)
```

```python
    def getRecentCount(self):
        return 0

    def isWriteable(self):
        return False

    def getUIDValidity(self):
        return self.uniqueValidityIdentifier

    def _seqMessageSetToSeqDict(self, messageSet):
        if not messageSet.last:
            messageSet.last = self.getMessageCount()

        seqMap = {}
        for messageNum in messageSet:
            if messageNum >= 0 and messageNum <= self.getMessageCount():
                seqMap[messageNum] = self.maildir[messageNum - 1]
        return seqMap

    def fetch(self, messages, uid):
        if uid:
            raise NotImplementedError(
                "This server only supports lookup by sequence number ")

        messagesToFetch = self._seqMessageSetToSeqDict(messages)
        for seq, filename in messagesToFetch.items():
            yield seq, MaildirMessage(file(filename).read())

    def addListener(self, listener):
        self.listeners.append(listener)

    def removeListener(self, listener):
        self.listeners.remove(listener)

class MaildirMessage(object):
    implements(imap4.IMessage)

    def __init__(self, messageData):
        self.message = email.message_from_string(messageData)

    def getHeaders(self, negate, *names):
        if not names:
            names = self.message.keys()

        headers = {}
        if negate:
            for header in self.message.keys():
                if header.upper() not in names:
                    headers[header.lower()] = self.message.get(header, '')
        else:
            for name in names:
                headers[name.lower()] = self.message.get(name, '')
```

```
            return headers

    def getBodyFile(self):
        return StringIO(self.message.get_payload())

    def isMultipart(self):
        return self.message.is_multipart()

class MailUserRealm(object):
    implements(portal.IRealm)

    def __init__(self, baseDir):
        self.baseDir = baseDir

    def requestAvatar(self, avatarId, mind, *interfaces):
        if imap4.IAccount not in interfaces:
            raise NotImplementedError(
                "This realm only supports the imap4.IAccount interface.")

        userDir = os.path.join(self.baseDir, avatarId)
        avatar = IMAPUserAccount(userDir)
        return imap4.IAccount, avatar, lambda: None

class IMAPServerProtocol(imap4.IMAP4Server):
    def lineReceived(self, line):
        print "CLIENT:", line
        imap4.IMAP4Server.lineReceived(self, line)

    def sendLine(self, line):
        imap4.IMAP4Server.sendLine(self, line)
        print "SERVER:", line

class IMAPFactory(protocol.Factory):
    def __init__(self, portal):
        self.portal = portal

    def buildProtocol(self, addr):
        proto = IMAPServerProtocol()
        proto.portal = portal
        return proto

log.startLogging(sys.stdout)

dataDir = sys.argv[1]

portal = portal.Portal(MailUserRealm(dataDir))
checker = checkers.FilePasswordDB(os.path.join(dataDir, 'passwords.txt'))
portal.registerChecker(checker)

reactor.listenTCP(1430, IMAPFactory(portal))
reactor.run()
```

To run this example, first create some content by running the SMTP server and client from the previous section, which will log messages to */tmp/mail*. Then create a */tmp/mail/passwords.txt* file with colon-delimited plain-text credentials for the recipients of those messages, as in:

```
recipient@localhost:pass
```

Run *python imapserver.py* to start the IMAP server listening on port 1430, authenticating based on the contents of */tmp/mail/passwords.txt*, and serving messages out of */tmp/mail*.

Next, we need an IMAP client to exercise this server.

IMAP Clients

Our minimal IMAP client will do the following:

1. Connect to an IMAP server.
2. List the mailboxes for the account.
3. Select a mailbox to examine.
4. Fetch all messages from that mailbox and print them to *stdout*.
5. Disconnect from the server.

To keep things simple, we'll only look for the Inbox mailbox. Example 13-5 implements this IMAP4 client task.

Example 13-5. IMAP client, imapclient.py

```python
from twisted.internet import protocol, reactor
from twisted.mail import imap4

USERNAME = 'recipient@localhost'
PASSWORD = 'pass'

class IMAP4LocalClient(imap4.IMAP4Client):
    def connectionMade(self):
        self.login(USERNAME, PASSWORD).addCallbacks(
            self._getMessages, self._ebLogin)

    def connectionLost(self, reason):
        reactor.stop()

    def _ebLogin(self, result):
        print result
        self.transport.loseConnection()

    def _getMessages(self, result):
        return self.list("", "*").addCallback(self._cbPickMailbox)
```

```
    def _cbPickMailbox(self, result):
        mbox = filter(lambda x: "Inbox" in x[2], result)[0][2]
        return self.select(mbox).addCallback(self._cbExamineMbox)

    def _cbExamineMbox(self, result):
        return self.fetchMessage('1:*', uid=False).addCallback(
            self._cbFetchMessages)

    def _cbFetchMessages(self, result):
        for seq, message in result.iteritems():
            print seq, message["RFC822"]

        return self.logout()

class IMAP4ClientFactory(protocol.ClientFactory):
    def buildProtocol(self, addr):
        return IMAP4LocalClient()

    def clientConnectionFailed(self, connector, reason):
        print reason
        reactor.stop()

reactor.connectTCP("localhost", 1430, IMAP4ClientFactory())
reactor.run()
```

Most of the IMAP queries are potentially expensive and thus return a Deferred to which
we attach callbacks to handle the result. The bulk of the work is done for us by
imap4.IMAP4Client's list, select, and fetchMessage methods.

With the IMAP server running, run the client to retrieve and print out all stored messages for *recipient@localhost* using the password *pass*. A server transcript might look
like this:

```
$ python imapserver.py /tmp/mail
2013-01-09 09:29:31-0500 [-] Log opened.
2013-01-09 09:29:31-0500 [-] IMAPFactory starting on 1430
2013-01-09 09:29:31-0500 [-] Starting factory <__main__.IMAPFactory instance at
  0x101706ab8>
2013-01-09 09:29:34-0500 [__main__.IMAPFactory] SERVER: * OK [CAPABILITY
  IMAP4rev1 IDLE NAMESPACE] Twisted IMAP4rev1 Ready
2013-01-09 09:29:34-0500 [IMAPServerProtocol,0,127.0.0.1] CLIENT: 0001
  CAPABILITY
2013-01-09 09:29:34-0500 [IMAPServerProtocol,0,127.0.0.1] SERVER: * CAPABILITY
  IMAP4rev1 IDLE NAMESPACE
2013-01-09 09:29:34-0500 [IMAPServerProtocol,0,127.0.0.1] SERVER: 0001 OK
  CAPABILITY completed
2013-01-09 09:29:34-0500 [IMAPServerProtocol,0,127.0.0.1] CLIENT: 0002 LOGIN
  "recipient@localhost" "pass"
2013-01-09 09:29:34-0500 [IMAPServerProtocol,0,127.0.0.1] SERVER: 0002 OK LOGIN
  succeeded
2013-01-09 09:29:34-0500 [IMAPServerProtocol,0,127.0.0.1] CLIENT: 0003 LIST ""
  "*"
```

```
2013-01-09 09:29:34-0500 [IMAPServerProtocol,0,127.0.0.1] SERVER: * LIST () "."
"Inbox"
2013-01-09 09:29:34-0500 [IMAPServerProtocol,0,127.0.0.1] SERVER: 0003 OK LIST
completed
2013-01-09 09:29:34-0500 [IMAPServerProtocol,0,127.0.0.1] CLIENT: 0004 SELECT
Inbox
2013-01-09 09:29:34-0500 [IMAPServerProtocol,0,127.0.0.1] SERVER: * 1 EXISTS
2013-01-09 09:29:34-0500 [IMAPServerProtocol,0,127.0.0.1] SERVER: * 0 RECENT
2013-01-09 09:29:34-0500 [IMAPServerProtocol,0,127.0.0.1] SERVER: * FLAGS ()
2013-01-09 09:29:34-0500 [IMAPServerProtocol,0,127.0.0.1] SERVER: * OK
[UIDVALIDITY 2612314]
2013-01-09 09:29:34-0500 [IMAPServerProtocol,0,127.0.0.1] SERVER: 0004 OK
[READ-ONLY] SELECT successful
2013-01-09 09:29:34-0500 [IMAPServerProtocol,0,127.0.0.1] CLIENT: 0005 FETCH 1:*
(RFC822)
2013-01-09 09:29:34-0500 [IMAPServerProtocol,0,127.0.0.1] SERVER: 0005 OK FETCH
completed
2013-01-09 09:29:34-0500 [IMAPServerProtocol,0,127.0.0.1] CLIENT: 0006 LOGOUT
2013-01-09 09:29:34-0500 [IMAPServerProtocol,0,127.0.0.1] SERVER: * BYE Nice
talking to you
2013-01-09 09:29:34-0500 [IMAPServerProtocol,0,127.0.0.1] SERVER: 0006 OK LOGOUT
successful
```

A client transcript might look like this:

```
$ python imapclient.py
1 Received: from localhost by 127.0.0.1 with ESMTP ; Wed, 09 Jan 2013 09:29:26
From: "Secret Admirer" <secretadmirer@example.com>
Content-Transfer-Encoding: 7bit
To: recipient@localhost
Mime-Version: 1.0
Content-Type: text/plain; charset="us-ascii"
Subject: Roses are red

Violets are blue
Twisted is helping
Forge emails to you!
```

POP3 Clients and Servers

The POP3 specification is defined in RFC 1939 (*http://bit.ly/XSB7Bt*).

For a taste of working with POP3, let's write a POP3 server that can serve the Maildir messages gathered by the SMTP client we created earlier, and a POP3 client to retrieve them.

POP3 Servers

A Twisted POP3 server will be structurally very similar to the IMAP server from the previous section. Twisted's `maildir` implementation actually uses POP3 mailbox semantics, so we have to write even less custom mailbox logic.

As with IMAP, we'll first need a protocol: in this case, a subclass of `twist ed.mail.pop3.POP3`. We'll also need a protocol factory subclassing `protocol.Factory` and building instances of our POP3 protocol. We can steal wholesale the `Realm`, `Portal`, and credentials checker from the IMAP server for authentication, thanks to Twisted Cred helping us keep our authentication logic decoupled from the business logic.

Example 13-6 shows a minimal POP3 server that serves mail out of the */tmp/mail maildir* directory structure we constructed with the SMTP server example.

Example 13-6. localhost POP3 server, pop3server.py

```python
import os
import sys
from zope.interface import implements

from twisted.cred import checkers, portal
from twisted.internet import protocol, reactor
from twisted.mail import maildir, pop3
from twisted.python import log

class UserInbox(maildir.MaildirMailbox):
    def __init__(self, userDir):
        inboxDir = os.path.join(userDir, 'Inbox')
        maildir.MaildirMailbox.__init__(self, inboxDir)

class POP3ServerProtocol(pop3.POP3):
    def lineReceived(self, line):
        print "CLIENT:", line
        pop3.POP3.lineReceived(self, line)

    def sendLine(self, line):
        print "SERVER:", line
        pop3.POP3.sendLine(self, line)

class POP3Factory(protocol.Factory):
    def __init__(self, portal):
        self.portal = portal

    def buildProtocol(self, address):
        proto = POP3ServerProtocol()
        proto.portal = self.portal
        return proto

class MailUserRealm(object):
    implements(portal.IRealm)

    def __init__(self, baseDir):
        self.baseDir = baseDir

    def requestAvatar(self, avatarId, mind, *interfaces):
```

```
        if pop3.IMailbox not in interfaces:
            raise NotImplementedError(
                "This realm only supports the pop3.IMailbox interface.")

        userDir = os.path.join(self.baseDir, avatarId)
        avatar = UserInbox(userDir)
        return pop3.IMailbox, avatar, lambda: None

log.startLogging(sys.stdout)

dataDir = sys.argv[1]

portal = portal.Portal(MailUserRealm(dataDir))
checker = checkers.FilePasswordDB(os.path.join(dataDir, 'passwords.txt'))
portal.registerChecker(checker)

reactor.listenTCP(1100, POP3Factory(portal))
reactor.run()
```

As before, to run this example, first create some content by running the SMTP server and client from the beginning of this chapter, which will log messages to */tmp/mail.* Then create a */tmp/mail/passwords.txt* file with colon-delimited, plain-text credentials for the recipients of those messages, for example:

```
    recipient@localhost:pass
```

Run *python pop3server.py* to start the POP3 server listening on port 1100, authenticating based on the contents of */tmp/mail/passwords.txt*, and serving messages out of */tmp/ mail.*

Next, we need a POP3 client to exercise this server. Example 13-7 demonstrates a client that will:

1. Connect to a POP3 server.

2. Get the sizes for the messages in the Inbox.

3. Retrieve each message and print it to *stdout.*

4. Disconnect from the server.

Example 13-7. POP3 client

```
from twisted.mail import pop3client
from twisted.internet import reactor, protocol, defer
from cStringIO import StringIO
import email

USERNAME = 'recipient@localhost'
PASSWORD = 'pass'

class POP3LocalClient(pop3client.POP3Client):
    def serverGreeting(self, greeting):
```

```
            pop3client.POP3Client.serverGreeting(self, greeting)
            login = self.login(USERNAME, PASSWORD).addCallbacks(
                self._loggedIn, self._ebLogin)

        def connectionLost(self, reason):
            reactor.stop()

        def _loggedIn(self, result):
            return self.listSize().addCallback(self._gotMessageSizes)

        def _ebLogin(self, result):
            print result
            self.transport.loseConnection()

        def _gotMessageSizes(self, sizes):
            retrievers = []
            for i in range(len(sizes)):
                retrievers.append(self.retrieve(i).addCallback(
                    self._gotMessageLines))
            return defer.DeferredList(retrievers).addCallback(
                self._finished)

        def _gotMessageLines(self, messageLines):
            for line in messageLines:
                print line

        def _finished(self, downloadResults):
            return self.quit()

class POP3ClientFactory(protocol.ClientFactory):
    def buildProtocol(self, addr):
        return POP3LocalClient()

    def clientConnectionFailed(self, connector, reason):
        print reason
        reactor.stop()

reactor.connectTCP("localhost", 1100, POP3ClientFactory())
reactor.run()
```

The bulk of the work is done for us by twisted.mail.pop3client's listSize and
retrieve methods. Both return Deferreds to which we attach callbacks to handle the
results.

With the POP3 server running, run this client to retrieve and print out all stored messages for *recipient@localhost* using the password *pass*. A server transcript might look
like this:

```
$ python pop3server.py /tmp/mail
2013-01-17 21:53:10-0500 [-] Log opened.
2013-01-17 21:53:10-0500 [-] POP3Factory starting on 1100
2013-01-17 21:53:10-0500 [-] Starting factory <__main__.POP3Factory instance
```

```
  at 0x10eaba3f8>
2013-01-17 21:53:11-0500 [__main__.POP3Factory] New connection from
 IPv4Address(TCP, '127.0.0.1', 49508)
2013-01-17 21:53:11-0500 [POP3ServerProtocol,0,127.0.0.1] CLIENT: CAPA
2013-01-17 21:53:11-0500 [POP3ServerProtocol,0,127.0.0.1] SERVER: TOP
2013-01-17 21:53:11-0500 [POP3ServerProtocol,0,127.0.0.1] SERVER: USER
2013-01-17 21:53:11-0500 [POP3ServerProtocol,0,127.0.0.1] SERVER: UIDL
2013-01-17 21:53:11-0500 [POP3ServerProtocol,0,127.0.0.1] SERVER: PIPELINE
2013-01-17 21:53:11-0500 [POP3ServerProtocol,0,127.0.0.1] SERVER: CELERITY
2013-01-17 21:53:11-0500 [POP3ServerProtocol,0,127.0.0.1] SERVER: AUSPEX
2013-01-17 21:53:11-0500 [POP3ServerProtocol,0,127.0.0.1] SERVER: POTENCE
2013-01-17 21:53:11-0500 [POP3ServerProtocol,0,127.0.0.1] SERVER: .
2013-01-17 21:53:11-0500 [POP3ServerProtocol,0,127.0.0.1] CLIENT: APOP
 recipient@localhost a0f3b61fb00f2473305886aec84ce358
2013-01-17 21:53:11-0500 [POP3ServerProtocol,0,127.0.0.1] Authenticated
 login for recipient@localhost
2013-01-17 21:53:11-0500 [POP3ServerProtocol,0,127.0.0.1] CLIENT: LIST
2013-01-17 21:53:11-0500 [POP3ServerProtocol,0,127.0.0.1] CLIENT: RETR 1
2013-01-17 21:53:11-0500 [POP3ServerProtocol,0,127.0.0.1] SERVER: .
2013-01-17 21:53:11-0500 [POP3ServerProtocol,0,127.0.0.1] CLIENT: QUIT
```

More Practice and Next Steps

This chapter introduced the Twisted Mail subprojects through simple but runnable SMTP, IMAP, and POP3 clients and servers.

The Twisted Mail HOWTO (*http://bit.ly/XSB5tk*) has an in-depth tutorial for building an SMTP client that can forward messages to a mail exchange server for delivery.

The Twisted Mail examples directory (*http://bit.ly/XSB7RZ*) has a collection of example clients and servers, including an authenticating SMTP client that communicates using Transport Layer Security (TLS).

CHAPTER 14

SSH

SSH, the *Secure SHell*, is an essential tool for many developers and administrators. SSH provides a way to establish encrypted, authenticated connections. The most common use of an SSH connection is to get a remote shell, but it's possible to do many other things through SSH as well, including transferring files and tunneling other connections.

The `twisted.conch` package adds SSH support to Twisted. This chapter shows how you can use the modules in `twisted.conch` to build SSH servers and clients.

SSH Servers

The command line is an incredibly efficient interface for certain tasks. System administrators love the ability to manage applications by typing commands without having to click through a graphical user interface. An SSH shell is even better, as it's accessible from anywhere on the Internet.

You can use `twisted.conch` to create an SSH server that provides access to a custom shell with commands you define. This shell will even support some extra features, like command history, so that you can scroll through the commands you've already typed.

A Basic SSH Server

To write an SSH server, implement a subclass of `twisted.conch.recvline.Histori cRecvLine` that implements your shell protocol. `HistoricRecvLine` is similar to `twist ed.protocols.basic.LineReceiver`, but with higher-level features for controlling the terminal.

To make your shell available through SSH, you need to implement a few different classes that `twisted.conch` needs to build an SSH server. First, you need the `twisted.cred` authentication classes: a portal, credentials checkers, and a realm that returns avatars.

Use `twisted.conch.avatar.ConchUser` as the base class for your avatar. Your avatar class should also implement `twisted.conch.interfaces.ISession`, which includes an `openShell` method in which you create a `Protocol` to manage the user's interactive session. Finally, create a `twisted.conch.ssh.factory.SSHFactory` object and set its `portal` attribute to an instance of your portal.

Example 14-1 demonstrates a custom SSH server that authenticates users by their username and password. It gives each user a shell that provides several commands.

To test this example, you'll need to generate a public key with an empty passphrase. The *OpenSSH* SSH implementation that comes with most Linux distributions and Mac OS X includes a command-line utility called *ssh-keygen* that you can use to generate a new private/public key pair:

```
$ ssh-keygen -t rsa
Generating public/private rsa key pair.
Enter file in which to save the key (/home/jesstess/.ssh/id_rsa):
Enter passphrase (empty for no passphrase):
Enter same passphrase again:
Your identification has been saved in /home/jesstess/.ssh/id_rsa.
Your public key has been saved in /home/jesstess/.ssh/id_rsa.pub.
The key fingerprint is:
6b:13:3a:6e:c3:76:50:c7:39:c2:e0:8b:06:68:b4:11 jesstess@kid-charlemagne
```

 Windows users that have installed Git Bash can also use *ssh-keygen*. You can also generate keys with PuTTYgen, which is distributed along with the popular free PuTTY SSH client (*http://bit.ly/XSB88p*).

Example 14-1. sshserver.py

```
from twisted.conch import avatar, recvline
from twisted.conch.interfaces import IConchUser, ISession
from twisted.conch.ssh import factory, keys, session
from twisted.conch.insults import insults
from twisted.cred import portal, checkers
from twisted.internet import reactor
from zope.interface import implements

class SSHDemoProtocol(recvline.HistoricRecvLine):
    def __init__(self, user):
        self.user = user

    def connectionMade(self):
        recvline.HistoricRecvLine.connectionMade(self)
        self.terminal.write("Welcome to my test SSH server.")
        self.terminal.nextLine()
        self.do_help()
        self.showPrompt()
```

```python
    def showPrompt(self):
        self.terminal.write("$ ")

    def getCommandFunc(self, cmd):
        return getattr(self, 'do_' + cmd, None)

    def lineReceived(self, line):
        line = line.strip()
        if line:
            cmdAndArgs = line.split()
            cmd = cmdAndArgs[0]
            args = cmdAndArgs[1:]
            func = self.getCommandFunc(cmd)
            if func:
                try:
                    func(*args)
                except Exception, e:
                    self.terminal.write("Error: %s" % e)
                    self.terminal.nextLine()
            else:
                self.terminal.write("No such command.")
                self.terminal.nextLine()
        self.showPrompt()

    def do_help(self):
        publicMethods = filter(
            lambda funcname: funcname.startswith('do_'), dir(self))
        commands = [cmd.replace('do_', '', 1) for cmd in publicMethods]
        self.terminal.write("Commands: " + " ".join(commands))
        self.terminal.nextLine()

    def do_echo(self, *args):
        self.terminal.write(" ".join(args))
        self.terminal.nextLine()

    def do_whoami(self):
        self.terminal.write(self.user.username)
        self.terminal.nextLine()

    def do_quit(self):
        self.terminal.write("Thanks for playing!")
        self.terminal.nextLine()
        self.terminal.loseConnection()

    def do_clear(self):
        self.terminal.reset()

class SSHDemoAvatar(avatar.ConchUser):
    implements(ISession)

    def __init__(self, username):
        avatar.ConchUser.__init__(self)
```

```python
        self.username = username
        self.channelLookup.update({'session': session.SSHSession})

    def openShell(self, protocol):
        serverProtocol = insults.ServerProtocol(SSHDemoProtocol, self)
        serverProtocol.makeConnection(protocol)
        protocol.makeConnection(session.wrapProtocol(serverProtocol))

    def getPty(self, terminal, windowSize, attrs):
        return None

    def execCommand(self, protocol, cmd):
        raise NotImplementedError()

    def closed(self):
        pass

class SSHDemoRealm(object):
    implements(portal.IRealm)

    def requestAvatar(self, avatarId, mind, *interfaces):
        if IConchUser in interfaces:
            return interfaces[0], SSHDemoAvatar(avatarId), lambda: None
        else:
            raise NotImplementedError("No supported interfaces found.")

def getRSAKeys():
    with open('id_rsa') as privateBlobFile:
        privateBlob = privateBlobFile.read()
        privateKey = keys.Key.fromString(data=privateBlob)

    with open('id_rsa.pub') as publicBlobFile:
        publicBlob = publicBlobFile.read()
        publicKey = keys.Key.fromString(data=publicBlob)

    return publicKey, privateKey

if __name__ == "__main__":
    sshFactory = factory.SSHFactory()
    sshFactory.portal = portal.Portal(SSHDemoRealm())

    users = {'admin': 'aaa', 'guest': 'bbb'}
    sshFactory.portal.registerChecker(
        checkers.InMemoryUsernamePasswordDatabaseDontUse(**users))

    pubKey, privKey = getRSAKeys()
    sshFactory.publicKeys = {'ssh-rsa': pubKey}
    sshFactory.privateKeys = {'ssh-rsa': privKey}

    reactor.listenTCP(2222, sshFactory)
    reactor.run()
```

sshserver.py will run an SSH server on port 2222. Connect to this server with an SSH client using the username *admin* and password *aaa*, and try typing some commands:

```
$ ssh admin@localhost -p 2222
admin@localhost's password: aaa
>>> Welcome to my test SSH server.
Commands: clear echo help quit whoami
$ whoami
admin
$ echo hello SSH world!
hello SSH world!
$ quit
Connection to localhost closed.
```

 If you've already been using an SSH server on your local machine, you might get an error when you try to connect to the server in this example. You'll get a message saying something like "Remote host identification has changed" or "Host key verification failed," and your SSH client will refuse to connect.

The reason you get this error message is that your SSH client is remembering the public key used by your regular *localhost* SSH server. The server in Example 14-1 has its own key, and when the client sees that the keys are different, it gets suspicious that this new server may be an impostor pretending to be your regular *localhost* SSH server. To fix this problem, edit your *~/.ssh/known_hosts* file (or wherever your SSH client keeps its list of recognized servers) and remove the *localhost* entry.

The SSHDemoProtocol class in Example 14-1 inherits from `twisted.conch.re cvline.HistoricRecvline`. `HistoricRecvLine` is a protocol with built-in features for building command-line shells. It gives your shell features that most people take for granted in a modern shell, including backspacing, the ability to use the arrow keys to move the cursor forwards and backwards on the current line, and a command history that can be accessed using the up and down arrows key. `twisted.conch.recvline` also provides a plain `RecvLine` class that works the same way, but without the command history.

The `lineReceived` method in `HistoricRecvLine` is called whenever a user enters a line. Example 14-1 shows how you might override this method to parse and execute commands. There are a couple of differences between `HistoricRecvLine` and a regular `Protocol`, which come from the fact that with `HistoricRecvLine` you're actually manipulating the current contents of a user's terminal window, rather than just printing out text. To print a line of output, use `self.terminal.write`; to go to the next line, use `self.nextLine`.

The `twisted.conch.avatar.ConchUser` class represents the actions available to an authenticated SSH user. By default, `ConchUser` doesn't allow the client to do anything. To make it possible for the user to get a shell, make the user's avatar implement `twisted.conch.interfaces.ISession`. The `SSHDemoAvatar` class in Example 14-1 doesn't actually implement all of `ISession`; it only implements enough for the user to get a shell.

The `openShell` method is called with a `twisted.conch.ssh.session.SSHSessionProcessProtocol` object that represents the encrypted client's end of the encrypted channel. You have to perform a few steps to connect the client's protocol to your shell protocol so they can communicate with each other:

1. Wrap your protocol class in a `twisted.conch.insults.insults.ServerProtocol` object. You can pass extra arguments to `insults.ServerProtocol`, and it will use them to initialize your protocol object.

   This sets up your protocol to use a virtual terminal.

2. Use `makeConnection` to connect the two protocols to each other.

   The client's protocol actually expects `makeConnection` to be called with an object implementing the lower-level `twisted.internet.interfaces.ITransport` interface, not a `Protocol`; the `twisted.conch.session.wrapProtocol` function wraps a `Protocol` in a minimal `ITransport` interface.

 The library traditionally used for manipulating a Unix terminal is called *curses*. The Twisted developers, never willing to pass up the chance to use a pun in a module name, therefore chose the name *insults* for this library of classes for terminal programming.

To make a realm for your SSH server, create a class that has a `requestAvatar` method. The SSH server will call `requestAvatar` with the username as `avatarId` and `twisted.conch.interfaces.IAvatar` as one of the interfaces. Return your subclass of `twisted.conch.avatar.ConchUser`.

To run the SSH server, create a `twisted.conch.ssh.factory.SSHFactory` object. Set its `portal` attribute to a portal using your realm, and register a credentials checker that can handle `twisted.cred.credentials.IUsernamePassword` credentials. Set the `SSHFactory`'s `publicKeys` attribute to a dictionary that matches encryption algorithms to keys.

Once the `SSHFactory` has the keys, it's ready to go. Call `reactor.listenTCP` to have it start listening on a port, and you've got an SSH server.

Using Public Keys for Authentication

The SSH server in Example 14-1 used usernames and passwords for authentication. But heavy SSH users will tell you that one of the nicest features of SSH is its support for key-based authentication. With key-based authentication, the server is given a copy of a user's public key. When the user tries to log in, the server asks her to prove her identity by signing some data with her private key. The server then checks the signed data against its copy of the user's public key.

In practice, using public keys for authentication is nice because it saves the user from having to manage a lot of passwords. A user can use the same key for multiple servers. She can choose to password-protect her key for extra security, or she can use a key with no password for a completely transparent login process.

To change the Twisted Cred backend for Example 14-1 to use public key authentication, store a public key for each user and write a credentials checker that accepts credentials implementing `twisted.conch.credentials.ISSHPrivateKey`. Verify the users' credentials by checking to make sure that their public keys match the keys you have stored and that their signatures prove that the users possess the matching private keys. Example 14-2 implements this checker.

Example 14-2. pubkeyssh.py

```
from sshserver import SSHDemoRealm, getRSAKeys
from twisted.conch import error
from twisted.conch.ssh import keys, factory
from twisted.cred import checkers, credentials, portal
from twisted.internet import reactor
from twisted.python import failure
from zope.interface import implements
import base64

class PublicKeyCredentialsChecker(object):
    implements(checkers.ICredentialsChecker)
    credentialInterfaces = (credentials.ISSHPrivateKey,)

    def __init__(self, authorizedKeys):
        self.authorizedKeys = authorizedKeys

    def requestAvatarId(self, credentials):
        userKeyString = self.authorizedKeys.get(credentials.username)
        if not userKeyString:
            return failure.Failure(error.ConchError("No such user"))

        # Remove the 'ssh-rsa' type before decoding.
        if credentials.blob != base64.decodestring(
            userKeyString.split(" ")[1]):
            raise failure.failure(
                error.ConchError("I don't recognize that key"))
```

```
    if not credentials.signature:
        return failure.Failure(error.ValidPublicKey())

    userKey = keys.Key.fromString(data=userKeyString)
    if userKey.verify(credentials.signature, credentials.sigData):
        return credentials.username
    else:
        print "signature check failed"
        return failure.Failure(
            error.ConchError("Incorrect signature"))

sshFactory = factory.SSHFactory()
sshFactory.portal = portal.Portal(SSHDemoRealm())

# The server's keys.
pubKey, privKey = getRSAKeys()
sshFactory.publicKeys = {"ssh-rsa": pubKey}
sshFactory.privateKeys = {"ssh-rsa": privKey}

# Authorized client keys.
authorizedKeys = {
    "admin": "ssh-rsa AAAAB3NzaC1yc2EAAAADAQABAAAAgQC2HXjFquK08rpEQC\
xLu/f4btDQ/2r3qRImVV/daKfQDu6QVm2P0BQ91Svyg60/VKxASqA1/PeN8Q0jSrdKcA\
By90KfkD2BCUk9gL0wCAfm8E5lNSbH54WY8l1XaUbQr+KitN1GSY/MgBvzqm5m7EdIHJ\
juX+54j4i0EEey46qJaQ=="
    }
sshFactory.portal.registerChecker(
    PublicKeyCredentialsChecker(authorizedKeys))

reactor.listenTCP(2222, sshFactory)
reactor.run()
```

To test this example, you'll need to generate a public key pair for the SSH client to use, if you don't have one already. You can generate a key using the same command from the previous example. Once you've generated a key, you can get the public key from the file *~/.ssh/id_rsa.pub*. Edit Example 14-2 to use your public key for the *admin* user in the *authorizedKeys* dictionary. Then run *pubkeyssh.py* to start the server on port 2222. You should log right in without being prompted for a password:

```
$ ssh admin@localhost -p 2222

>>> Welcome to my test SSH server.
Commands: clear echo help quit whoami
$
```

If you try to log in as a user who doesn't possess the matching private key, you'll be denied access:

```
$ ssh bob@localhost -p 2222
Permission denied (publickey).
```

Example 14-2 reuses most of the SSH server classes from Example 14-1. To support public key authentication, it uses a new credentials checker class named PublicKeyCredentialsChecker. PublicKeyCredentialsChecker accepts credentials implementing ISSHPrivateKey, which have the attributes username, blob, signature, and sigData. To verify the key, PublicKeyCredentialsChecker goes through three tests. First, it makes sure it has a public key on file for credentials.username. Next, it verifies that the public key provided in blob matches the public key it has on file for that user.

It's possible that the user may have provided just the public key at this point, but not a signed token. If the public key was valid but no signature was provided, PublicKeyCredentialsChecker.requestAvatar raises the special exception twisted.conch.error.ValidPublicKey. The SSH server will understand the meaning of this exception and ask the client for the missing signature.

Finally, we use the key's verify method to check whether the data in the signature really is the data in sigData signed with the user's private key. If verify returns True, authentication is successful and requestAvatarId returns username as the avatar ID.

 You can support both username/password and key-based authentication in an SSH server. Just register both credentials checkers with your portal.

Providing an Administrative Python Shell

Example 14-1 demonstrated how to provide an interactive shell through SSH. That example implemented its own language with a small set of commands. But there's another kind of shell that you can run over SSH: the same interactive Python prompt you know and love from the command line.

The twisted.conch.manhole and twisted.conch.manhole_ssh modules have classes designed to provide a remote interactive Python shell inside your running server. Example 14-3 demonstrates a web server that can be modified on the fly using SSH and twisted.conch.manhole.

Example 14-3. manholeserver.py

```
from twisted.internet import reactor
from twisted.web import server, resource
from twisted.cred import portal, checkers
from twisted.conch import manhole, manhole_ssh

class LinksPage(resource.Resource):
    isLeaf = 1

    def __init__(self, links):
        resource.Resource.__init__(self)
```

```
        self.links = links

    def render(self, request):
        return "<ul>" + "".join([
            "<li><a href='%s'>%s</a></li>" % (link, title)
            for title, link in self.links.items()]) + "</ul>"

links = {'Twisted': 'http://twistedmatrix.com/',
         'Python': 'http://python.org'}
site = server.Site(LinksPage(links))
reactor.listenTCP(8000, site)

def getManholeFactory(namespace, **passwords):
    realm = manhole_ssh.TerminalRealm()
    def getManhole(_): return manhole.Manhole(namespace)
    realm.chainedProtocolFactory.protocolFactory = getManhole
    p = portal.Portal(realm)
    p.registerChecker(
        checkers.InMemoryUsernamePasswordDatabaseDontUse(**passwords))
    f = manhole_ssh.ConchFactory(p)
    return f

reactor.listenTCP(2222, getManholeFactory(globals(), admin='aaa'))
reactor.run()
```

manholeserver.py will start up a web server on port 8000 and an SSH server on port 2222. Figure 14-1 shows what the home page looks like when the server starts.

Figure 14-1. The default manholeserver.py web page

Now log in using SSH. You'll get a Python prompt, with full access to all the objects in the server. Try modifying the links dictionary:

```
$ ssh admin@localhost -p 2222
admin@localhost's password: aaa
>>> dir()
    ['LinksPage', '__builtins__', '__doc__', '__file__', '__name__', 'checkers',
     'getManholeFactory', 'links', 'manhole', 'manhole_ssh', 'portal', 'reactor',
     'resource', 'server', 'site']
```

```
>>> links
{'Python': 'http://python.org', 'Twisted': 'http://twistedmatrix.com/'}
>>> links["Django"] = "http://djangoproject.com"
>>> links["O'Reilly"] = "http://oreilly.com"
>>> links
{'Python': 'http://python.org', "O'Reilly": 'http://oreilly.com', 'Twisted':
'http://twistedmatrix.com/', 'Django': 'www.djangoproject.com'}
>>>
```

Then refresh the home page of the web server. Figure 14-2 shows how your changes will be reflected on the website.

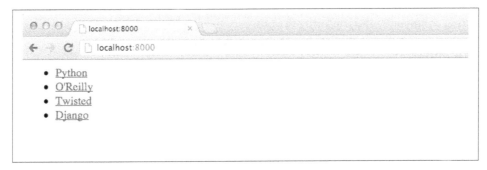

Figure 14-2. Modified manholeserver.py web page

Example 14-3 defines a function called getManholeFactory that makes running a manhole SSH server trivially easy. getManholeFactory takes an argument called name space, which is a dictionary defining which Python objects to make available, and then a number of keyword arguments representing usernames and passwords. It constructs a manhole_ssh.TerminalRealm and sets its chainedProtocolFactory.protocolFac tory attribute to an anonymous function that returns manhole.Manhole objects for the requested namespace. It then sets up a portal using the realm and a dictionary of usernames and passwords, attaches the portal to a manhole_ssh.ConchFactory, and returns the factory.

Note that passing a dictionary of Python objects as namespace is strictly for convenience (to limit the set of objects the user has to look through). It is *not* a security mechanism. Only administrative users should have permission to use the manhole server.

Example 14-3 creates a manhole factory using the built-in globals function, which returns a dictionary of all the objects in the current global namespace. When you log in through SSH, you can see all the global objects in *manholeserver.py*, including the *links* dictionary. Because this dictionary is also used to generate the home page of the website, any changes you make through SSH are instantly reflected on the Web.

The manhole_ssh.ConchFactory class includes its own default public/private key pair. For your own projects, however, you shouldn't rely on these built-in keys. Instead, generate your own and set the publicKeys and privateKeys attributes of the ConchFactory. See Example 14-1, earlier in this chapter, for an example of how to do this.

Running Commands on a Remote Server

You can use twisted.conch to communicate with a server using SSH: logging in, executing commands, and capturing the output.

SSH Clients

There are several classes that work together to make up a twisted.conch.ssh SSH client. The transport.SSHClientTransport class sets up the connection and verifies the identity of the server. The userauth.SSHUserAuthClient class logs in using your authentication credentials. The connection.SSHConnection class takes over once you've logged in and creates one or more channel.SSHChannel objects, which you then use to communicate with the server over a secure channel. Example 14-4 shows how you can use these classes to make an SSH client that logs into a server, runs a command, and prints the output.

Example 14-4. sshclient.py

```python
from twisted.conch.ssh import transport, connection, userauth, channel, common
from twisted.internet import defer, protocol, reactor
import sys, getpass

class ClientCommandTransport(transport.SSHClientTransport):
    def __init__(self, username, password, command):
        self.username = username
        self.password = password
        self.command = command

    def verifyHostKey(self, pubKey, fingerprint):
        # in a real app, you should verify that the fingerprint matches
        # the one you expected to get from this server
        return defer.succeed(True)

    def connectionSecure(self):
        self.requestService(
            PasswordAuth(self.username, self.password,
                        ClientConnection(self.command)))

class PasswordAuth(userauth.SSHUserAuthClient):
    def __init__(self, user, password, connection):
        userauth.SSHUserAuthClient.__init__(self, user, connection)
```

```python
        self.password = password

    def getPassword(self, prompt=None):
        return defer.succeed(self.password)

class ClientConnection(connection.SSHConnection):
    def __init__(self, cmd, *args, **kwargs):
        connection.SSHConnection.__init__(self)
        self.command = cmd

    def serviceStarted(self):
        self.openChannel(CommandChannel(self.command, conn=self))

class CommandChannel(channel.SSHChannel):
    name = 'session'

    def __init__(self, command, *args, **kwargs):
        channel.SSHChannel.__init__(self, *args, **kwargs)
        self.command = command

    def channelOpen(self, data):
        self.conn.sendRequest(
            self, 'exec', common.NS(self.command), wantReply=True).addCallback(
            self._gotResponse)

    def _gotResponse(self, _):
        self.conn.sendEOF(self)

    def dataReceived(self, data):
        print data

    def closed(self):
        reactor.stop()

class ClientCommandFactory(protocol.ClientFactory):
    def __init__(self, username, password, command):
        self.username = username
        self.password = password
        self.command = command

    def buildProtocol(self, addr):
        protocol = ClientCommandTransport(
            self.username, self.password, self.command)
        return protocol

server = sys.argv[1]
command = sys.argv[2]
username = raw_input("Username: ")
password = getpass.getpass("Password: ")
factory = ClientCommandFactory(username, password, command)
reactor.connectTCP(server, 22, factory)
reactor.run()
```

Run *sshclient.py* with two arguments: a hostname and a command. It will ask for your username and password, log into the server, execute the command, and print the output. For example, you could run the *who* command to get a list of who's currently logged in to the server:

```
$ python sshclient.py myserver.example.com who
    Username: jesstess
    Password: password
    root     pts/0          Jun 11 21:35 (192.168.0.13)
    phil     pts/2          Jun 22 13:58 (192.168.0.1)
    phil     pts/3          Jun 22 13:58 (192.168.0.1)
```

The `ClientCommandTransport` class in Example 14-4 handles the initial connection to the SSH server. Its `verifyHostKey` method checks to make sure the server's public key matches your expectations. Typically, you'd remember each server the first time you connected and then check on subsequent connections to make sure that another server wasn't maliciously trying to pass itself off as the server you expected. Here, it just returns a `True` value without bothering to check the key.

The `connectionSecure` method is called as soon as the initial encrypted connection has been established. This is the appropriate time to send your login credentials, by passing a `userauth.SSHUserAuthClient` to `self.requestService`, along with a `connection.SSHConnection` object that should manage the connection after authentication succeeds.

The `PasswordAuth` class inherits from `userauth.SSHUserAuthClient`. It has to implement only a single method, `getPassword`, which returns the password it will use to log in. If you wanted to use public key authentication, you'd implement the methods `getPublicKey` and `getPrivateKey` instead, returning the appropriate key as a string in each case.

The `ClientConnection` class in Example 14-4 will have its `serviceStarted` method called as soon as the client has successfully logged in. It calls `self.openChannel` with a `CommandChannel` object, which is a subclass of `channel.SSHChannel`. This object is used to work with an authenticated channel to the SSH server. Its `channelOpen` method is called when the channel is ready.

At this point, you can call `self.conn.sendRequest` to send a command to the server. You have to encode data sent over SSH as a specially formatted *network string*; to get a string in this format, pass it to the `twisted.conch.common.NS` function. Set the keyword argument `wantReply` to `True` if you're interested in getting a response from the command; this setting will cause `sendRequest` to return a `Deferred` that will be called back when the command is completed. (If you don't set `wantReply` to `True`, `sendRequest` will return None.) As data is received from the server, it will be passed to `dataReceived`. Once you're done using the channel, close it by calling `self.conn.sendEOF`. The `closed` method will be called to let you know when the channel has been successfully closed.

More Practice and Next Steps

This chapter introduced the Twisted Conch subproject through example SSH clients and servers. Some of the examples utilized *insults*, Twisted's terminal control library. Others utilized the *twisted.conch.manhole* module for introspecting and interacting with a running Python process.

The Twisted Conch HOWTO (*http://bit.ly/XSB5JS*) walks through implementing an SSH client. Prolific Twisted Core developer JP Calderone walks through implementing an SSH server in his "Twisted Conch in 60 Seconds" (*http://bit.ly/XSB5K1*) series.

The Twisted Conch examples (*http://bit.ly/XSB60q*) include an *insults*-based drawing application, a Python interpreter with syntax highlighting, a *telnet* server, and scrolling.

CHAPTER 15

The End

We've reached the end of our tour through the Twisted library.

We started with an overview of Twisted's architecture and the event-driven programming model. We practiced using Twisted's primitives and common idioms to write basic clients and servers, and then built up and deployed production-grade servers that log, authenticate, talk to databases, and more. We finished by surveying client and server implementations for several popular protocols.

You now have all of the tools you need to build and deploy event-driven clients and servers for any protocol, and I think you'll find that to be a powerful tool to have in your back pocket. Twisted powers everything from networked game engines and streaming media servers to web crawling frameworks and continuous integration systems to Bit-Torrent clients and AMQP peers. The next time you need to programmaticaly download data from a website, test an HTTP client, process your email, or annoy your friends with an IRC bot, you know what to do.

Thank you for reading! We'd love to hear your thoughts on this book. Please send feedback and technical questions to *bookquestions@oreilly.com*. You can find more information about the book, and a list of errata, at *http://oreil.ly/twisted-network-2e*.

Contributing to Twisted

Twisted exists because of the collective effort of dozens of core developers and hundreds of contributors. For over a decade, they have volunteered their time to the library and sourrounding infrastructure. Please join us in improving Twisted.

There are many ways to help: writing code, documentation, and tests; maintaining the website and build infrastructure; and helping users on the mailing lists and IRC. Join the `twisted-python` mailing list or `#twisted-dev` IRC channel on Freenode (*http://freenode.net/*), say hello, and we'll help you get started!

Index

A

adbapi
    switching from blocking API to, 77–79
    using with SQLite, 78
addBoth method, 36, 56
addCallback method, 26, 31–35, 36
addCallbacks method, 27–28, 33–35, 36
addErrback method, 27–27, 31–35, 36
administrative Python shell, SSH providing, 153–155
Agent API, 53, 55–60
agent.request, 56
AlreadyCalledError, 35
ampoule, 101
API
    Agent, 53, 55–60
    blocking, 77–79, 93
    Deferred, 36, 50, 50
        (see also Deferreds)
    platform-independent, 96
    producer/consumer, 58
    threading, 101
API documentation, using Twisted, 8–8
applications, deploying Twisted, 63–69
Applications, in Twisted application infrastructure, 64
Ascher, David, Learning Python, xvi
asynchronous code
    about using Deferreds in, 25

addCallback method vs. addErrback method, 33–35
keyfacts about Deferreds, 35
managing callbacks not registered, 25
structure of Deferreds, 26–28
structuring, 25
using callback chains inside of reactor, 28–29
using callback chains outside of reactor, 26–28
asynchronous headline retriever, 28
asynchronous responses, web server, 49–51
authentication
    in Twisted applications, 89–90
    using public keys for, 151–153, 158
authentication, using Cred
    about, 81
    chat-specific, 121–124
    components of, 81–82
    examples of, 82–86
    process in, 84
AuthOptionMixin class, 89–91
AutobahnPython, Web-Sockets implementation, 22
avatar ID, definition of, 82
avatar, definition of, 81

B

blocking API, 77–79, 93
blockingApiCall, 95

We'd like to hear your suggestions for improving our indexes. Send email to index@oreilly.com.

blockingCallFromThread method, 96
blogs, for Twisted, 9
browsers
    GET request, 42
    serializing requests to same resource, 51
buildProtocol method, 16, 85, 130

C

C compiler, installing, 5
Calderone, JP, "Twisted Conch in 60 Seconds"
    series, 158
callback chains
    in Deferreds, 26–28
    using inside of reactor, 28–29
    using outside of reactor, 26–28
callbacks
    attaching to non-blocking database queries,
        78, 79
    attaching to writeSuccessResponse, 97
    Deferreds using outside of reactor, 26–28
    failing to register, 25
    practice using, 30–31
    registering multiple, 27–28
callFromThread method, 96
callInThread method, 93
callLater method, 29, 108, 112
callMultipleInThread method, 96
channelOpen method, 158
ChatFactory, 21, 106
ChatProtocol states, 21
chatserver, testing, 106–108
client, 142
    (see also web client)
    communication in Twisted, 19
    IRC, 119–121
    POP3, 142
    simultaneous connections to server, 19
    SMTP, 127–129, 143
    SSH, 156–158
    TCP echo, 11–16
ClientCommandTransport class, 158
ClientConnection class, 158
clients
    IMAP, 137–139
closed method, 158
ColorizedLogObserver, 74
commands standard library module, 96–100
conchFactory, manhole_ssh, 155
ConchUser class, 149

connection.SSHConnection class, 156
connectionLost method, 15, 56
connectionMade method, 15, 98, 99
connectionSecure method, 158
connectTCP method, 14
Cred authentication system
    about, 81
    chat-specific, 121–124
    components of, 81–82
    examples of, 82–86
    process in, 84
    SSH server, 145–146
credentialInterfaces class variable, 87
credentialInterfaces, authenticating, 85
credentials checkers
    database-backed, 87–88
    DBCredentialsChecker, 87–88, 110–112
    definition of, 82
    FilePasswordDB, 86
    IMAP, 133
    in UNIX systems, 91
    POP3, 139
    returning Deferred to Portal, 85
    SSH server, 145–146, 153
credentials, definition of, 81
curses library, 150

D

DailyLogFile class, 73
data, streaming large amounts of, 58
databases, non-blocking queries, 77–79
dataReceived method, 15, 56
dataReceived methods, IProtocol interface, 20
DBCredentialsChecker, 87–88, 110–112
decoupling, transports and protocols, 16
deferLater method, 94
Deferreds
    about Deferred API, 36
    agent.request returning, 56
    asynchronous responses on web server us-
        ing, 50
    credentials checker to Portal, 85
    in non-blocking database queries, 78, 79
    keyfacts about, 35
    POP3 client returning, 142
    practice using, 30–35
    shutting down reactor before firing, 95
    testing, 109–112
    using callback chains inside of reactor, 28–29

About the Authors

Jessica McKellar is a software engineer from Cambridge, Massachusetts. She enjoys the Internet, networking, low-level systems engineering, and contributing to and helping other people contribute to open source software. She is a Twisted maintainer, organizer for the Boston Python user group, and a local STEM volunteer.

Abe Fettig is a software developer and maintainer of Hep, an open source message server that makes it possible to transparently route information between RSS, email, weblogs, and web services. He speaks frequently at software conferences including PyCon and lives in Portland, Maine with his wife, Hannah.

Colophon

The image on the cover of *Twisted Network Programming Essentials*, 2nd Edition shows a ball of snakes. When the ground begins to thaw in spring, things heat up for some species of snakes. Males emerge from their hibernation dens cold, hungry, and randy! An estimated 50,000 male snakes can fill a location such as a limestone quarry, waiting patiently for nearby females to emerge. When they do, the mating frenzy begins, and it can last up to three weeks.

As many as 100 to 1,000 males will compete to mate with a single female, sometimes surrounding her before she can fully emerge from her den. The males wrap around the female, becoming a living ball that can grow to be two feet high. The constant writhing of the snakes can even propel the ball over rocks and tree roots.

In some cases, the size of the snake ball will crush the female to death. However, this does not always deter the males, who may continue to mate with her.

A female will normally mate with only one male in the ball; once a male has successfully copulated with her, he releases a pheromone that temporarily makes all other males in the ball impotent. When the female selects her partner, the ball unravels and the unsuccessful males go in search of another female.

Since it is difficult for snakes to determine the gender of their potential partner, males detect the female by using their flicking tongues to sense the female's pheromones, which stimulate the males to mate. The male rubs his chin against the grain of the female's scales to squeeze out her pheromones. It is believed that the male can also determine the position of the female by detecting the direction of her pheromones and then aligning himself with her body accordingly.

The cover image is from a 19th-century engraving from the Dover Pictorial Archive. The cover font is Adobe ITC Garamond. The text font is Adobe Minion Pro; the heading font is Adobe Myriad Condensed; and the code font is Dalton Maag's Ubuntu Mono.

Get even more for your money.

Join the O'Reilly Community, and register the O'Reilly books you own. It's free, and you'll get:

- $4.99 ebook upgrade offer
- 40% upgrade offer on O'Reilly print books
- Membership discounts on books and events
- Free lifetime updates to ebooks and videos
- Multiple ebook formats, DRM FREE
- Participation in the O'Reilly community
- Newsletters
- Account management
- 100% Satisfaction Guarantee

Signing up is easy:

1. **Go to: oreilly.com/go/register**
2. **Create an O'Reilly login.**
3. **Provide your address.**
4. **Register your books.**

Note: English-language books only

To order books online:
oreilly.com/store

For questions about products or an order:
orders@oreilly.com

To sign up to get topic-specific email announcements and/or news about upcoming books, conferences, special offers, and new technologies:
elists@oreilly.com

For technical questions about book content:
booktech@oreilly.com

To submit new book proposals to our editors:
proposals@oreilly.com

O'Reilly books are available in multiple DRM-free ebook formats. For more information:
oreilly.com/ebooks

O'REILLY®

Spreading the knowledge of innovators   oreilly.com

Have it your way.

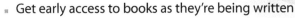